THE ENGLISH RANKE:
JOHN LINGARD

From a painting by James Ramsay.

John Lingard

THE ENGLISH RANKE:
JOHN LINGARD

by

DONALD F. SHEA

HUMANITIES PRESS

New York   1969

TABLE OF CONTENTS

PREFACE

The almost flood of historiographical studies that have appeared particularly in the last decade invites company. David Hume, James Anthony Froude, Frederic William Maitland, Lord Acton— these and many other English historians have had their day. The absence, by contrast, of the man whose history remained, in Gooch's estimate, "the most popular sketch of our history till the appearance of Green" attracted my attention.

This study of John Lingard has been made possible by a double generosity. First was the interest and aid of the late Monsignor Philip Hughes, distinguished historian of the Church and disciple of Lingard, who made available to me some two hundred of the historian's unpublished letters. Second was the financial aid and sabbatical grant of Saint Joseph's College; these permitted first-hand research and travel in the "Lingard country" of northern England.

D. F. Shea

Rensselaer, Indiana
July 24, 1968

THE ENGLISH RANKE:
JOHN LINGARD

CHAPTER I

ACROSS TWO CENTURIES

The eighty years of John Lingard's life, 1771 to 1851, witnessed profound and dramatic changes in almost every facet of English life. George III was young and sane when Lingard was born; Victorian was already becoming an adjective when he died. Toryism was still unchallenged in those years before the American revolt; Lord John Russell and Palmerston set the Liberal tone of the fifties. When John Lingard was born Louis XV and du Barry still ruled at Versailles; the Old Regime, by 1851, was three revolutions and many rulers away. The rejuvenated English mercantilism of the 1770's had largely surrendered to Peel's free trade. Watt's steam engine, from an untried novelty, was rapidly transforming the whole fabric of English life. Classicism in painting, architecture, and literature had, by the time of Lingard's death, given way to Turner's landscapes, the Gothic revival, and Dickens.

Yet of all the aspects and facets of Lingard's times, two must be especially considered in the proximate setting of John Lingard the historian: the historiographical and the religious. For to evaluate this writer of history the general contemporary condition of historical writing must be known. No less, to understand this English Catholic priest who wrote history, the issues and men in contemporary English Catholicism must be recalled.

1. The Historiographical Setting

The first half of the nineteenth century witnessed changing interpretations and philosophies among English historians. What the dominant tone of the preceding century had been there is little doubt: English historians and historical writing had been rationalistic in philosophy and Tory in politics. These historiographical traits, however, were but reflections of the broader characteristics of the dominant Enlightenment. David Hume (1711-1776),

1

William Robertson (1721-1793) and Edward Gibbon (1737-1794) expressed in their histories only the skepticism and naturalism, the toryism, of their day. Nor were these men oblivious of their biases; Hume wrote of his *History of England,* "I may be liable to the reproach of ignorance, but I am certain to escape that of Impartiality."

The weaknesses of eighteenth century historical writing may be summarized as four.[1] First and most basic was the intrinsic repugnance of the Enlightenment to the past. The universal law of human perfectability was far more attractive than scholarly, painstaking research. Hume dismissed the Anglo-Saxon era as a time of kites and crows, but characterized Alfred as a perfect model of all that is great and good. Robertson's and Gibbon's contempt for religious feeling and motives is well known. A second obstacle to historical writing in the later Enlightenment was not new to that period: the continued lack of original, authentic documents. The view of governmental records as public was still to come. Closely associated with this disability was the continuing lack of true criticism in using what sources were available. Dugald Stewart, a minor historian of the late eighteenth century, only reflected his times when he suggested that lack of "direct historical evidence" justified creating a new species of philosophical investigation which he would call "theoretical or conjectural history" to account for the present happily high "intellectual acquirements."[2]

As a final unfavorable characteristic of historical writing in the age of Hume and Gibbon, the almost total lack of the teaching of history must be noted. George I did, it is true, establish chairs of modern history at both the great universities, but seldom did their holders, among whom was the poet Gray, bother to lecture.[3]

---

1. Cf., e.g., George P. Gooch, *History and Historians in the Nineteenth Century,* rev. ed. (London, 1952), pp. 10-12.
2. Dugald Stewart, "The Life and Writings of Adam Smith, LL.D.," in *Works of Adam Smith* (London, 1811), V, p. 450.
3. The classics and mathematics, together with some formalized theology, quite filled the curricula of the English universities in the eighteenth century. History, as such, extended only to the study of the classics; modern history seems never to have been taught at either of the great universities. Arthur Gray, *Cambridge University: an Episodal History* (Boston, 1927), p. 225.

The lesser historical lights of the later eighteenth century, Adam Ferguson (1723-1816), Joseph Priestley (1733-1804), and John Reeves (1752?-1829), no less than the greater, were characteristically rationalistic and tory.

During the opening decades of the nineteenth century, however, fundamental and far-reaching changes were occurring in English historiography. The rationalistic, classical bias of the previous age was giving way to one characteristically romantic. The toryism of Hume was being replaced by the whiggism of Turner, Hallam, and Macaulay. The Enlightenment's disdain for much of the past, and the partially consequent dearth of historical sources, began to be corrected with the establishment of the Record Commission in 1800, although it did little until 1838, when Francis Palgrave was appointed to it. But its foundation can be taken to symbolize the gradually changing attitude towards historical sources. No less significant was the appointment in 1819 as Keeper of Records in the Tower of London of Henry Petrie (1768-1842), who later instigated the movement that resulted in the *Rolls*.

More important, though, than individual contemporary historians, was the spirit or philosophy that commonly pervaded them: what outlook and viewpoint did they generally share? The historical atmosphere of those decades of Lingard's productive life was dominated by what came to be known as the whig interpretation of history.[4] Although this term has come to include some rather definite elements, many of them are evident no less in other historical schools or movements. Yet together they distinguish the whig historian. Herbert Butterfield has ably epitomized this viewpoint or philosophy of some historians: "to write on the side of Protestants and Whigs, to praise revolutions provided they have been successful, to emphasize certain principles of progress in the past and to produce a story which is the ratification if not the glorification of the present." Or even more pointedly, "Whig

---

4. Particularly valuable for their analyses of whig history are Herbert Butterfield. *The Whig Interpretation of History* (London, 1950), who rightly cautions that it is "not a problem in the philosophy of history, but rather an aspect of the psychology of historians"; and R. W. K. Hinton, "History Yesterday," *History Today*, IX (November, 1959), pp. 720-728.

history is a story of fortunate development achieved by steps that were intrinsically correct."

It is part and parcel of the whig interpretation of history that it studies the past with reference to the present. Of all the characteristics of the whig historian this is perhaps the most fundamental; it furnished him with a ready, although ultimately unhistorical, principle of selection of historical facts and judgments. It becomes, at least implicitly, his criterion for evaluating the significance of past events and historical persons.

Though it is surely true that the "roots of the present lie deep in the past," yet to study the latter only with the eyes and mind of the former is just as surely to endanger the historical outlook and objectivity. For although Lord Morely might declare that "the life of the nineteenth century strikes its roots in the thirteenth," still the politics of John Stewart Mill in the mind of the historian obscures and distorts the historical King John.

Sharon Turner's (1768-1847) chief work, *History of the Anglo-Saxons*, presented the early Teutons primarily as founders and precursors of his own England. "Our language, our government, and our laws display our Gothic ancestors in every part. They live, not merely in our annals and traditions, but in our civil institutions and perpetual discourse." Similarly, one of Lingard's immediate successors, George Grote (1794-1871), viewed and evaluated the political development of ancient Greece from the standpoint of a nineteenth century English liberal.

A second quality of the Whig historian is his sympathy, in varying degrees pronounced or implicit, with what might generally be termed political liberalism. The growth of civil and religious "freedom," as conceived by the nineteenth century liberal, form for him one of the main currents of historical development. The upward progress from shackles to individual liberty culminates, to the historian of this persuasion, in the liberal atmosphere of his own day.[5] Although a distinction is often at least implied between allegiance to whig principles on the one hand and to the Whig

---

5. Cf., e.g., George Bancroft, "The Necessity, the Reality, and the Promise of the Progress of the Human Race," New York Historical Society *Proceedings* (New York, 1854), pp. 10-18.

party on the other, even the latter more usually finds the favor. See, for example, Macaulay's unashamed devotion: "I entered public life a Whig and a Whig I still remain. . . . Whatever has been done for the amelioration of the condition of the people, for the modification of the penal laws, has been done by that party, and of that party, I repeat, I am a member." To the Whigs Macaulay anachronistically credited opposition to Elizabeth, Parliamentary strength under James I, and the abolition of ship-money under his son.[6] This was, of course, in large part but a natural reaction to the contrary tory history which had prevailed in the preceding century. Still at the end of the nineteenth century Lord Acton could make the core of his historical studies the history of freedom.

In the same vein, Gooch says simply of Henry Hallam's (1777-1859) *Constitutional History of England,* "Written while the Tory domination was still unbroken, it constituted a political manifesto. . . . At the moment when the Reform Bill inaugurated a generation of Whig politics, he inaugurated a generation of Whig history." Why, in spite of Hallam's general fidelity to sources and his relatively careful scholarship, he can so unqualifiedly be termed a whig in historiography is evident from this typical dictum: "The Whigs appear to have taken a far more comprehensive view of the nature and ends of civil society: their principle is more virtuous, more flexible to the variations of time and circumstance, more congenial to large and masculine intellects." He concludes his eulogy of the Glorious Revolution by saying plainly, "I consider the Revolution to have been eminently conducive to our freedom and prosperity."

Closely associated with this sympathy for political liberalism is the whig historian's basically Protestant, or perhaps better, anti-clerical, outlook. To him the Reformation was a movement of religious liberals emancipating man from Catholic intellectual and spiritual repression, and preparing the way to nineteenth century freedom. Trevelyan's *History of England,* for example, has been characterized as a "gentleman's version of the Protestant

---

6. Thomas Babington Macaulay, *The History of England from the Accession of James II* (New York, 1868), I, pp. 48-49, 69.

tradition." Earlier, Robert Southey (1774-1843), though writing as an historian in his *Book of the Church*, was fundamentally a controversialist, attacking Catholic repression of individual and moral freedom. Among Lingard's successors, James Anthony Froude (1818-1894) was thoroughly the whig historian when he wrote of the English Reformation: "The wonderful growth in wealth and social energy in Elizabeth's England was accompanied and caused by a remarkable change in the religious temper of the nation: it was in these years that England became firmly Protestant." Similarly, Edward Freeman (1823-1892), in his monumental *Norman Conquest*, viewed the medieval Church as the opponent of religious and individual liberty: "The Conqueror . . . taught men to argue that, if the Roman Pontiff could rightly be called on to judge between two claimants of the English Crown, he might also be rightly called on to judge between the wearer of that Crown and his own subjects." Today, indeed, "Froude's disease" and Freeman's prejudices are proverbial.

Another trait of whig history, flowing from the more basic views already noted, is the general tendency to be concerned with ultimate judgments, moral and political, on historical persons and events. Again it was perhaps Acton in whom the moral value of history is clearest: "It is the office of historical science to maintain morality as the sole impartial criterion of men and things." But the morals and values of the whig historian are always those of his own day: liberal and Protestant. Hence wars and rebellions, battles and men are judged significant in so far as they contributed to or hindered the coming of the political and religious order of the nineteenth century.

Examples abound. George Bancroft (1800-1891), Lingard's leading American contemporary historian, seemed often more the judge and arbiter of the past than its historical narrator. "The hour of the American revolution was come. . . . The Americans seized their peculiar inheritance, the traditions of liberty." Similarly, the whiggism of Froude permitted him to eulogize the despoilers of the monasteries in the 1530's as those who "deprive the idol of its terrors by daring to defy it."

These fundamental traits of whig history bring with them two other characteristics. First, in combination, they are "bound to lead to an over-dramatization of the historical story." The very fact that the whig historian more easily and willingly sees relations and associations of past events and causes with present ones quite naturally prompts him to portray the former more vividly and sympathetically. What may, in its historical context, have had but slight contemporary significance may be dramatized out of proportion because of its possible affinity with a present circumstance or conviction. Macaulay's vivid portrayal of Warren Hastings gives perhaps undue prominence to a man and event not proportionally significant. But after all, Macaulay had once said that,

> History, at least in its state of ideal perfection is the compound of poetry and philosophy. It impresses general truths on the mind by vivid representations of particular characters or incidents.[7]

The dramatic qualities of John Richard Green's description of England at the time of Elizabeth's accession reveals his penchant for the striking generalization:

> Never had the fortunes of England sunk to a lower ebb than at the moment when Elizabeth mounted the throne. The country was humiliated by defeat, and brought to the verge of rebellion by the bloodshed and misgovernment of Mary's reign. The old social discontent, trampled down for a time by the mercenary troops of Somerset, still remained a perpetual menace to public order. The religious strife had passed beyond hope of reconciliation, now that the Reformers were parted from their opponents by the fires of Smithfield, and the party of the New Learning all but dissolved. The Catholics were bound helplessly to Rome. Protestantism, burned at home and hurled into exile abroad, had become a fiercer thing; and was pouring back from Geneva with dreams of revolutionary change in Church and State. England,

---

7. Thomas Babington Macaulay, *Works*, ed. by Lady Trevelyan (London, 1879), V, p. 162.

dragged at the heels of Philip into a useless and ruinous war, was left without an ally save Spain; while France, mistress of Calais, became mistress of the Channel. Not only was Scotland a standing danger to the north, through the French marriage of Mary Stuart and its consequent bondage to French policy; but its queen had assumed the style and arms of an English sovereign, and threatened to rouse every Catholic throughout the realm against Elizabeth's title. In presence of this host of dangers the country lay utterly helpless, without army or fleet, or the means of maintaining one; for the treasury, already drained by the waste of Edward's reign, had been utterly exhausted by Mary's restoration of the Church-lands, and by the cost of her war with France. England's one hope lay in the character of her queen.[8]

A second effect of whig principles in historical writing is the tendency to generalizations and broad interpretations. Prior and unsuppressed convictions on political and religious liberty, the function of history, and the place of values in it, make trends and movements, progress and retrogression far clearer and more evident. The epigram, the happy phrase, the incisive interpretation come more easily. "Simple patterns are easier to understand than complicated ones, and carry more conviction." Yet it is likewise true of the whig historian that "his own view of the course of history has provided him with those sympathies that waken imagination."

Perhaps only an historian of whig principles would have written *The History of Freedom* so as to "descry dimly the Declaration of Independence in the forests of Germany," or could have so clearly seen in ancient Athens a precursor of liberal England, or have detected connecting ancient and modern Sicily a real continuity, or have seen the Anglo-Saxon constitution, though hazy in detail, clear in outline.[9]

---

8. John Richard Green, *A Short History of the English People* (New York, 1880), p. 375.
9. In order: Lord Acton, George Grote, Edward A. Freeman, and Henry Hallam.

Whereas whiggism was the hallmark of English historical writing when Lingard's works began to appear, the historiographical tone on the continent was more mixed. There, amid lingering philosophical syntheses as well as nationalistic and romantic interest in sources occasioned especially by the French Revolution and Napoleon, the beginnings of the celebrated German critical method were emerging.

The great critical collection of German sources, the *Monumenta Germaniae Historica*, associated with Stein and Pertz, was inaugurated in 1819, the year when the first volume of Lingard's *History* appeared. Ten years later the French counterpart, the École des Chartes, was founded and the first of the Documents Inédits was published in 1826. Only François Michaud (1767-1839), famous for his *History of the Crusades*, was truly contemporary with Lingard among the great French romantic, national historians: Michelet, Thierry, Mignet. Meanwhile, Johann Herder (1744-1803) was reflecting the lingering Enlightenment's interest in philosophical synthesis while pioneering romantic idealism.

It was at the University of Göttingen in the late eighteenth century, however, and in Barthold Niebuhr (1776-1831), that continental historiography provided the most meaningful setting for Lingard. At Göttingen particularly Johann Gatterer (1727-99) was already demonstrating that distinctive German interest in universal history combined with source criticism. Only, however, with Niebuhr's *History of Rome* in 1811-12 did the new, critical method make its unquestioned impact; this pioneer work united a romantic interest in origins with textual criticism of Roman sources. Is it possible that even the detached, scholarly Niebuhr was whiggish in outlook? For even he wrote that, "The ever-growing perfection of the British constitution and freedom since 1688 affords the noblest picture of collective national wisdom and virtue that history can offer."

Leopold von Ranke (1795-1886) belongs to the next generation.[10] Not until 1824, with his first work, the *History of the Latin*

---

10. Cf. below, chapter VI.

and Germanic Peoples, did he begin to adapt and extend Niebuhr's critical principles to the broader field of European history. By this time, Lingard's initial work was largely finished.

This was the historical world of John Lingard. He had as his English contemporaries historians generally of the whig persuasion. On the continent, romanticism and nationalism numbered many historical converts. It was against this background that he published his first two volumes of history, *The Antiquities of the Anglo-Saxon Church,* in 1806. From 1819 to 1830 appeared the eight volumes of his *History of England,* and before his death in 1851, he prepared four additional editions of this work.

ii. The Religious Setting

When John Lingard was born, English Catholicism was at its nadir; when he died there was an English cardinal at Westminster presiding over a restored hierarchy. Christopher Hollis has suggested a graphic and convenient chronology of English Catholicism since the Reformation: from 1533 until the last Jacobite Revolt of 1745, Catholics, though decreasing, were still an important minority; but in the following century, until Newman's conversion in 1845, "Catholicism dropped out of English life." Even Bishop Challoner, for example, although venerated by Catholics of his own and later days, can scarcely be said to have played a truly national role in the wider setting of Hanoverian England. "For Catholics this was a period of dispirited discouragement."

Yet in 1778 the trend to Catholic civil emancipation began. In that year, under the general influence of fashionable tolerance and urged by the desire to secure the enlistment of Catholic Highlanders for service in the wars in the colonies and with France, Lord North's government carried through the first Catholic Relief Act. Eleven years later the second Catholic bill became law, so that, for the first time in 232 years it was no longer a penal act to say Mass in England. That full emancipation was only a question of time was clear. George III, its stolid opponent, was growing older; the thousands of French Catholic emigrees in

England and the sympathy for the Catholic Bourbons aided their English co-religionists.

To English Catholicism at the turn of the nineteenth century, persecution from without was less foreboding and threatening than division within. During the latter half of the preceding century, what may be considered a descendant of Gallicanism, modified to suit the century and country, became firmly rooted among English Catholics. Political accommodation to English government, insistence on only the dogmatically essential Catholic teachings and practices, a reduction of external ceremonial pomp: these distinguished the English Cisalpines.

These accommodating, liberal views were thrown into bold relief by the government's repeated efforts to obtain guarantees from the Catholics as to the papal deposing power as well as some kind of governmental veto in the appointment of Catholic bishops. Especially the first of these issues English Catholics of the late eighteenth century seemed willing to repudiate to a dangerous degree. "The Gallican leaven . . . and the idea of the point of honor imparted a slight unreality to moral questions." The basic similarity on many points of the Cisalpine Catholic and the whig historian will become evident later.

Urged by their changing political fortunes and by the necessity for definitively clarifying their stand on certain basic issues, a group of English Catholics was forming in opposition to the dominant Cisalpine attitude. Ultramontanism, although the term is more characteristic of the mid-century, already stood for deep attachment to the Holy See, not only in basic dogma, but also in papal discipline and organization. It held fast to the essentially defensive view of English Catholics as a necessarily isolated minority.

Restrained and necessarily cautious though early English Ultramontanism might have been, its loyalty to Rome and unashamed devotion to the Church forcibly contrasted with the far more conciliatory Cisalpinism.

In the opening three decades of the nineteenth century two men came to symbolize these two opposing camps among English Catholics. Charles Butler was the moving force of the lay Catholic

Committee, the core of Cisalpine opinion. His direct opposite, a man congenitally unable to compromise, was Bishop John Milner, Vicar-Apostolic of the Midlands District. With both John Lingard had long and frequent associations. With whom he was in closer personal accord there can be no doubt. Whether this personal affinity extended into the realms of political and religious doctrine and attitude will be considered later.

John Lingard, during the last quarter century of his life, was witness to two outstanding events in the English Catholic revival. In 1829 the Catholic Relief Act granted the long-awaited emancipation. In 1850 Pius IX restored the national hierarchy, with Nicholas Wiseman as cardinal-archbishop of Westminster and twelve suffragan bishoprics. But during the intervening twenty-one years two other developments were occurring. The Catholic population of England increased more than two-fold, from 200,000 to a half-million, while its center was shifting from country to city. Simultaneously, the Oxford Movement was giving to the Church notable converts and intellectual respectability. These factors combined to allow Newman to see a Second Spring. Just as Lingard's relations to Butler and Milner reveal his own position, so do his associations with the leaders of 1850.

John Lingard, the English priest-historian, was himself an historical figure, linking Hume with Green, Challoner with Wiseman. The eighty year span of his life saw both the birth and growth of English historical criticism and the second birth, as it were, of English Catholicism.

CHAPTER II

THE VICAR OF HORNBY

A full, balanced biography necessarily looks at every facet of its subject. The purpose here is far more restricted: what were the factors and events that stimulated in John Lingard his interest in history and that influenced his writing of it? What were the biographical elements that contributed to John Lingard the historian? There is, in this matter, considerable justification for the comment of Lingard's first biographer, Canon Tierney: "It has been frequently, and not unnaturally, remarked that the history of an author's life is little more than the history of his works." For to know Lingard's writings, their origins, qualities, and successes, is to know, to a goodly extent, their author.

Winchester, the old Catholic center of northern Lincolnshire where John Lingard was born in 1771, was well suited to be a historian's birthplace. The very neighborhood of Jarrow and Weremouth recalled the memory of Bede; Lindisfarne and Hexham remained living antiquities. Indeed, directly opposite the old Lingard home stood the twelfth century church of St. Mary, which by the eighteenth century was Anglican.

Lingard's mother, Elizabeth Rennell, was of an old family of recusants in the Catholic center around Winchester. His father's religious antecedents are less certain: the older tradition, adopted by Gillow, held that Ralph Lingard, like his master, Squire Markham of Claxby, was also a recusant. But during the last century the local tradition was that Lingard was a convert to his wife's Catholicism.

Mrs. Lingard, after her son had become famous, wrote the memoirs of her life. Although the manuscript has since been lost, it was used by Canon Tierney for his *Memoir*. He quotes Mrs. Lingard as saying that she could always "keep John quiet" by giving him a history book, and that she "searched the neighborhood" for any work of history that could be found.[1] Until he left for Douai at the age of eleven, his mother recalled that her son "was accustomed to hire books, particularly historical ones, which he seemed eager to peruse." Interestingly, the priest resident at Winchester during part of Lingard's boyhood, who had encouraged him in his studies, was his later antagonist, John Milner.

One of Bishop Challoner's last acts was to grant a burse for John Lingard at Douai College. Almost fifty years later, preparing for his second trip to Rome, Lingard longed to revisit his alma mater.[2] Still at the age of seventy-seven, he recalled "30 September, 1782, a boy called John Lingard entered the portals of Douai College. *Deo Gratias*."[3] The deep tradition and historical atmosphere of this "Catholic England beyond the Seas" served to encourage Lingard's interest in history.

After eight years of preparatory and college work, Lingard, on June 3, 1790, took the famous "College Oath." With it, he joined as one of the last, the missionaries of Douai:

> I, ..., an Alumnus of the English College at Douai, . . . promise and swear before Almighty God that I am ready, and will be ever ready, to receive Holy Orders in due time, and to return to England in order to gain the souls of others as often and when it shall seem good to the Superior of this College so to command.

At the same time, the president of Douai, William Gibson, described Lingard as "*Juvenis undequaque optimae spei, Ingenior, Studio, et Pietate pariter commendabilis.*"

Lingard began his course in theology in October, 1791, in an atmosphere hardly conducive to detached scholarship. The town of Douai was subject to all the whims and violence of revolutionary France. Twice Lingard secretly witnessed the execution of two of the local clergy, and once had literally to run for his own life.

---

1. Michael A. Tierney, "Memoir of Rev. Dr. Lingard," in John Lingard, *A History of England from the First Invasion by the Romans to the Accession of William and Mary in 1688*, 6th ed. (London, 1855), I, p. 1.
2. MS., to Joseph Mawman, May, 1825.
3. September 30, 1847, in Martin Haile and Edwin Bonney, *Life and Letters of John Lingard, 1771-1851* London, 1911), p. 19.

Finally, one month after the execution of Louis XVI, Lingard with three other students, left for England.

By contemporary standards, the course in humanities, as it was called, at Douai, was a good one. The studies were almost exclusively classical; history and mathematics were omitted. Charles Butler, a fellow student of Lingard, recalled, "The Classics were well taught, but . . . writing, arithmetic, and geography were little regarded; modern history was scarcely mentioned." As if the political agitation was not sufficient distraction from his theological training, Lingard, during his last two years at Douai, taught students in the second year of college. In all, then, Lingard spent eleven years at Douai, 1782-1793, the last two of which were in theology.

After a lapse in his studies of over a year, during which Lingard acted as tutor for Lord Stourton's sons, he resumed his theology at Crook Hall at Durham. He arrived in August, 1794, and, his theology still uncompleted, was appointed acting vice-president, professor of moral and natural philosophy, as well as of rhetoric and poetry, prefect of studies, and procurator. Nor were these the only obstacles to a solid grounding in theology; books were so scarce that each student had to write out all his work before he could study it. After only four months of theology under these conditions, John Lingard was ordained deacon; and on April 18, 1795, he was raised to the priesthood. In view of Lingard's theological training, his views later in life of the papal deposing power or of liturgical functions, indeed, what might be called his "theological timidity," can hardly cause wonder.

For almost two decades, until he was appointed rector of Hornby in 1811, Lingard remained at Ushaw, as Crook Hall was known after 1803. Here at Durham, "where the very stones cried out their messages of the past, . . . Lingard's passion for the antiquities of his country had full play." Tierney, quoting from the records and memories of Lingard's fellow professors, says,

> In moments snatched from the various duties of his office, he embodied in a series of detached papers his thoughts on the establishment of the faith among the Saxons, the

origins of the monastic institute, the government of the
Church, of the learning, literature, and laws of Anglo-
Saxon times. . . . Seated with his friends around the
glowing coal-fires he read these papers in the evening
hours.

As the reader advanced, the interest of the audience
grew more intense: The extent of his reading and the
depth of his research struck them at once with surprise
and admiration: and when, at length, the series drew to
a close, they united with one accord in urging him to
mould the detached parts into a regular form, and publish
them as a connected history. For a long time, his diffidence
or his modesty withstood the application.[4]

During a few months in the year 1800 Lingard kept a journal.
Although only fragments remain, they reveal his broadening his-
torical reading and research. Gibbon he read thoroughly, and then
Fleury, Froissart, Villani, and Muratori. Even in these early years,
Lingard began to build up his core of historical correspondents in
England and on the continent. Charles Butler sent transcripts of
Anglo-Saxon manuscripts, of which there is still preserved at
Ushaw *The Chronicles of England* from 730 to 1058 and the
eighth century *Pontifical of Egbert*.

In November, 1806, appeared John Lingard's first two volumes
of history, the *Antiquities of the Anglo-Saxon Church*. Bishop
Milner, Charles Butler, Sharon Turner, John Allen, and the Irish
bishops all took note of the new history and historian.[5] Lingard
would be for the next forty-five years among the foremost
historians of England. In 1810 a second edition was called for and
again, thirty-five years later, Lingard, then seventy-five years old,
revised and enlarged his first historical work.

In 1811, partially as a result of clerical bickerings, and partially
because of his desire for a post affording more time for reading and
research Lingard left Ushaw. He came to the village with which
his name was forever to be linked: for forty years, until his death

---

4. Tierney, "Memoir," pp. 14-15.
5. Cf. below, chapter V.

in 1851, Dr. Lingard was "vicar of Hornby," as he styled himself.[6] Hornby, lying in the valley of the Lune, eight miles from Lancaster, had a population of 420, forty of whom were Catholics. Even today the topography, the little village, the comfortable house and classic chapel are inviting and picturesque. They were surely pleasant changes from the relative bleakness of Durham.

Here, far removed from the literary and ecclesiastical centers of England, one of the most eminent men of his age lived out his life. Seldom, indeed, towards the end not at all, did the "vicar" venture from it. Yet the isolation, though making research more difficult, was not without its advantages. For one, Hornby very possibly preserved Lingard from succumbing to the changing literary fashions of London, so allowing his style to remain simpler and less dated. For another, the seclusion encouraged the learned rector to read even more voluminously and voraciously.[7] His research, reading, parochial calls on the sick all notwithstanding, Lingard admitted to his publisher, "The truth is I find these long winter evenings long and dull, and am anxious to know what is going on in the world."[8]

Difficult to reach though it was, in those days of poor roads, Hornby became a mecca for many of the political and literary leaders of England. During the Lancaster Assizes the three prominent Whig lawyers, Henry Brougham, Jonathan Pollock, and James Scarlett came regularly to Hornby. These, with Dr. Lingard and the Unitarian ministry from Gatacre, near Liverpool, William Shepard, formed the "Hornby circle."[9] Brougham's elevation to the peerage in 1830 caused this original group to change, but the bar of the Northern Circuit continued to visit the priest-historian,

---

6. The title, more usually applied to the Anglican clergy, was first playfully applied to Lingard by the Anglican minister at Hornby.
7. MSS., to Joseph Mawman, November 3 and November 14, 1825.
8. MS., to Joseph Mawman, December, 1825.
9. Sir Jonathan Pollock (1783-1870) was a leading barrister of the day, and "though place cannot be claimed for him among the most illustrious of the sages of the law, he yields to none in the second rank." James Scarlett (1769-1844) "was neither a great lawyer nor an eloquent speaker, and yet he was by far the most successful advocate of his day." William Shepherd (1768-1847) was a close friend of Edward Wakefield and a prison reformer in his own right. Of the group Lord Brougham was, of course, by far the most renowned.

and in 1834, had James Lonsdale paint Lingard's portrait. Francis Jeffrey, the first editor of the *Edinburg Review*, Thomas Jerdon, editor of the *Literary Gazette*, William Wright, the antiquary, Thomas Pettigrew, the surgeon, and the painters Allan Ramsay and Samuel Lovers made the pilgrimage. The political unanimity of the Hornby visitors is noteworthy: they were, quite without recorded notable exception, Whig. Notable too is the fact that they were, in great majority, non-Catholics.

The *Times*, in Lingard's obituary, was able to state, "Such a thing as a religious feud was never heard of during the whole 40 years he lived at Hornby."[10] His life evidently reflected what he wrote to his publisher, "A man who loses his temper is not fit to conduct a cause of consequence."[11] Of the Catholic rector's local popularity there is no better testimony than the tablet which the Protestants of Hornby erected in the Anglican church:

> In memory of John Lingard, D.D.
> the learned author of the History of England
> and of the Antiquities of the Anglo-Saxon Church.
> He died at Hornby xviii July MDCCCLI
> Aged 82 [sic]
> and was buried at Ushaw College Durham.
> 'Quis desideric sit—Modus Tam cari capitis?'
> This tablet is erected by his friends and associates.

Prominent also among his non-Catholic acquaintances were Wordsworth and Southey, both of whom, in 1834, Lingard instructed on the manner of acting as witnesses in the local court.

When Lingard came to Hornby in 1811 he had already made the first beginnings on what was to be the great work of his life, the *History of England*. His *Anglo-Saxon Church* had initiated him into historical method and writing, and had convinced him of the necessity of factual rather than the prevalent philosophical history. In 1809, while still at Ushaw, both Charles Butler and Joseph Coyne, the Dublin publisher, approached Lingard. The former had two quite divergent suggestions: First he urged Lin-

---

10. London *Times*, July 28, 1851, p. 7.
11. MS., to Joseph Mawman, August 29, 1827.

gard to write a history of the Anglo-Norman church, so continuing his first work. Then in the same year, speaking for the Catholic Committee, the core of Cisalpine sentiment, Butler tried to interest the historian in editing, or at least contributing to, a proposed periodical that would be the organ for the anti-Milner group. At the same time the Irish publisher Coyne, was writing to Lingard:

> Let me know, have you yet finished your abridgement of English History for the use of schools? . . . A small volume would, I think, take in Ireland, and leave the poisoned Goldsmith to Protestant schools. If you can with convenience abridge the English History to about 400 pages twelves, I think I shall amply compensate you for your labor.[12]

This, then, was the proximate origin of Lingard's *History*. He at first thought merely of a relatively brief school text, correcting the errors and prejudices of previous writers. The more ample time at his disposal during his first years at Hornby allowed him gradually to expand his purpose to writing an original, general history of England. By 1813 he had written an outline history of England to 1485 and was making notes correcting especially Hume, Robertson, and Turner. For the next five years the rector of Hornby worked on what was to be the opening volumes of his *History*. So busy was he that he had to refuse John Kirk's request to contribute to the new *Catholic Gentleman's Magazine*.

After unsuccessfully offering the manuscript of the first volumes to two Catholic publishers, Booker and Keating, Lingard contacted Joseph Mawman:

> I had sent about 300 pages, which he submitted to the inspection of Lord Holland, Mr. Brougham, and Mr. Allen: and after hearing their report, consented to give my demands, viz. 1000 guineas. On the condition that I would let him have the second part, not yet written, he added 500 to be paid me on the second edition of the first part. The second he is to have on the same condition

12. MS., from Joseph Coyne, December, 1809.

as the first, in proportion to its extent. It is not a bad bargain.[13]

The retail price for the three volumes was to be five guineas, the equivalent today of ten times that amount. Nonetheless, in the first two weeks after the volumes were published, 500 copies were sold.

These first three volumes of the *History of England* ended with the death of Henry VII. The following year the fourth volume was published, and in 1823 the fifth. These caused even greater interest outside the Church and controversy within for they treated the crucial sixteenth century. The final three volumes carried the *History* to its conclusion with the flight of James II in 1688.

Before his death two decades later, Lingard prepared four additional editions (1823-1831, 1825, 1839, and 1849-1851), of which the fifth was most important because of the new material it incorporated. Lingard was eighty years of age when he completed it. In addition to these two major writings, the *Antiquities* and the *History*, Dr. Lingard's published works number no less than thirty-one, and his articles in periodicals exceed thirty.

The first money that Lingard received from his *History* he used, in 1822, for a new chapel at Hornby, the cost of which was greater than he expected, so that in March of that year he wrote, "Till I receive my dividends in May I must contrive to live without money and upon credit, for I am *quasi* without a shilling. By 1839, however, he had an average annual income of about £400, of which £150 was from his charge at Hornby. At the time of his death, the *History* in its five editions, had brought him a total of between £8000 and £9000. This was a happy change from his early years at Hornby, when his meager funds prevented him from buying even many basic sources.[14]

Lingard's historical labors brought him not only a comfortable income but also notable honors, both in Rome and in England. While his *History of England* was still uncompleted, Pius VII on

---

13. MS., to Robert Gradwell, April 18, 1818.
14. MS., to John Kirk, January 27, 1818.

August 24, 1822, by a special brief, conferred upon the historian the triple honorary degrees of doctor of divinity, and of civil and canon law. In the same year, the pontiff ordered the *History* to be translated into Italian and printed on the presses of the Propaganda. Too, the English priest was elected a member of the Accademia di Religione Cattolica of Rome.

Lingard found no less favor, and indeed greater intimacy, with Pope Leo XII (1823-1829). Writing in a facetious vein in 1840 to his friend John Walker, who had said that he possessed a candle of Leo XII, Lingard said:

> There is something in that candle that calls for veneration: but that he is too blind to perceive. It came from Leo XII, the greatest pontiff that Rome has seen since the days of St. Peter. Why so? Because he was the only one who has ever had the sagacity to discover the transcendent merit of J. L. He patronized my work, he defended my character against the slanders of Padre Ventura and the fanatics, he made me a cardinal *in petto*, he described me in his consistory as not one of the servile *pecus* of historians, but one who offered the world *historiam ex ipsis haustam fontibus.* Are not all these feathers in his cap, jewels in his tiara?[15]

It was Leo XII, who, in the consistory of October, 1826, created four cardinals, in addition to several *reservati in petto*. The Holy Father described one of the latter as a man of great talents and scholarship, whose writings, drawn from original sources, *ex nativis fontibus*, had delighted Europe. Whether John Lingard was the cardinal *in petto* was discussed heatedly but unsatisfactorily. Dr. Gradwell, the rector of the English College in Rome, assured Lingard that he was the man.[16] Cardinal Wiseman, thirty years later, flatly rejected the claim, endorsing, rather, Lammenais.

---

15. MS., to John Walker, September 14, 1840.
16. MSS., to Joseph Mawman, January 20, 1827; and to John Bradley, January 27, 1829.

Regardless of the correct solution, that Lingard's name figured so prominently in the speculation testifies to his fame in Rome.[17]

However, that Lingard was offered a bishopric on at least two occasions there is no doubt. In 1817 Bishop Peter Collingride, Vicar-Apostolic of the Western District, a Franciscan, wanted a coadjutor from the secular clergy, and through Bishop Poynter, approached Lingard. Poynter reported the latter's reaction:

> . . . Mr. Lingard said it would be a great impediment to the execution of his work, which he is anxious to bring to perfection and which the Catholic public is in great expectation of. He added that some of his reflections would not become the responsible character of a Bishop.— This is the substance of his objections. I now leave him to your Lordship.[18]

Four years later, when Thomas Smith, Vicar-Apostolic of the Northern District, sent Lingard's name to Rome as his coadjutor, the rector of Hornby, for the same reasons, showed himself even more unreceptive. Finally, in 1844, when Lingard was seventy-three, the rectorship of the English College at Rome was vacant, and the cardinal-protector inquired if the historian would accept the post. He replied plainly, "No, for I am unable to travel twenty miles from home."[19]

In his own country, too, Dr. Lingard was accorded honors seldom in his day granted to a Catholic priest. In 1824 he was elected an honorary associate of the new Royal Society of Literature. Fifteen years later, Melbourne's Whig administration granted the historian £300 from the Queen's privy purse. On both occasions Lingard noted that men of all parties were included, and that the Society was established "on most liberal principles." For neither honor did he apply or campaign.[20]

Lingard's position in English Catholic clerical circles was not

---

17. The most recent study of the problem is W. J. Hegarty, "Was Lingard a Cardinal?" *Irish Ecclesiastical Record*, LXXIX (February, 1953), pp. 81-93, though cautious, seriously questions whether Lingard was the pontiff's choice.
18. August 16, 1817, in Haile and Bonney, *Life and Letters*, p. 156.
19. MS., to John Walker, April 13, 1844.
20. MS., to Robert Gradwell, November 15, 1824.

commensurate with his fame in Rome or his renown as a historian. It is true, as we have seen, that several of the vicars-apostolic wished to elevate him to the episcopacy. Too, Bishop Poynter of London looked upon Lingard not only as a close friend but as, in the 1820's his "chief adviser," particularly concerning the historical and legal preparation for the 1829 Catholic Emancipation Act.[21] Also, Cardinal Acton wrote for Lingard's opinion on the method of selecting English bishops. Yet Bishop John Milner's violent denunciations of Lingard's works as excessively liberal and Cisalpine, and Lingard's known friendship with Charles Butler as well as his unflagging opposition to greater episcopal power and control in England lessened his influence among the English clergy. Significantly perhaps, during all his years at Hornby, Lingard seems not to have been invited to preach at any occasion outside his own church, not even at the funeral of his particularly intimate friend, Bishop Poynter.

To gain some insight into Lingard and his life, it should be remembered that John Lingard was himself an historical figure of an age of transition; he, who received one of the last burses granted by Bishop Challoner at Douai, lived to see the restoration of the English hierarchy. Yet this priest-historian lived most of his life in pre-emancipation England, when Catholicism was still a political and social stigma. The influence, however tacit or subtle, of his fifty-eight pre-emancipation years on his outlook and writings must not be overlooked. His season was not the Second Spring. Lingard, as virtually any writer or public figure, was at least to a degree, a man of his times. To what extent he was an insular Englishman will be considered later.

---

21. MSS., to Bishop William Poynter, March 18 and March 31, 1821.

CHAPTER III

MOTIVES: A MAN OF DOUAI

An investigation of an historian and his work necessarily involves the question of motive. Was John Lingard primarily, by purpose, an apologist employing history, or a disinterested historian having no more ultimate motive? Even to conclude the former is not necessarily to deny the possibility of his veracity and accuracy. For the problem here concerns the motives impelling this Catholic priest to write history, not the results. His purposes, not his products, are our concern at the moment. First we shall consider Lingard as an historian who wrote history for the sake of truth, devoid of more ultimate, pragmatic motives. Then, in partial contrast, as it were, we shall examine the statements of Lingard, of his contemporaries, and of his more recent critics, which combine to portray him as essentially an apologist. In this matter, too, we must gather as evidence his views concerning the place of Catholics in English life, as well as his characteristic manner or approach in presenting his history.

i. "My object is truth . . ."

In the preface to his first volume of history, *The Antiquities of the Anglo-Saxon Church*, Lingard regretted the sectarian controversy that had permeated not only popular literature but also the "learned" since the reformation. History had been prostituted by religious controversialists. In this framework he posed his famous question: "My object is truth; and in the pursuit of truth I have made it a religious duty to consult the original historians. Who would draw from the troubled stream, when he may drink at the fountain head?"[1] This clear awareness of the primacy of original sources, coming in 1806, must stand as an historiographical land-

---

1. John Lingard, *The Antiquities of the Anglo-Saxon Church* (Newcastle, 1806), I, p. vi.

mark. It precedes by more than a generation Leopold von Ranke's more famous insistence on original documents. Here Lingard appears, by his own statement, the disinterested scholar, seeking historical truth for its own sake. In 1819, as the opening volume of the *History* was published, the author wrote privately that, "Through the work, I made it a rule to tell the truth whether it made for or against us."[2] Almost forty years later, after he had repeatedly been criticized for failing explicitly to defend the Catholic position, Lingard repeated his concern with the historical fact as such: "With the truth or falsehood of doctrine the following pages have no concern; their object is to discover and establish facts."[3] Surely this goal is not far from Ranke's.

In 1823, for the second edition of his *History of England*, Lingard wrote a new, brief preface:

> . . . It can matter little what were the motives, which induced me to undertake the work. . . . It is long since curiousity first led me to consult the original writers; and an intimate acquaintance with these authorities convinced me, that if much had already been accomplished, yet much remained to be done; that in the best of our histories, there were errors to be corrected and omissions to be supplied; and that on several important subjects new information might be brought forward, to elucidate what was obscure, and to rectify what had been misrepresented.[4]

Here the historian sets up truth as his goal more by omitting mention of any more partisan, apologetic motives than by explicit statement. But he had good reason for caution: Bishop Milner, on the one hand, in his *Orthodox Journal*, was accusing his coreligionist of near heresy; John Allen, in the *Edinburgh Review*, on the other

---

2. MS., to John Kirk, December 18, 1819.
3. John Lingard, *The History and Antiquities of the Anglo-Saxon Church,* 2nd ed. (London, 1845), I, p. viii.
4. John Lingard, *A History of England from the First Invasion by the Romans to the Accession of William and Mary in 1688,* 5th ed. (Boston, 1854), I, xxiii-xxiv.

hand, was declaring Lingard to be a clever propagandist for Rome.[5]

Lingard's contemporary critics, even the most favorable, furnish meager evidence to portray him as a wholly disinterested searcher for truth. They may praise the accuracy and exactness of his products, but they question the purity of his purpose. For example, the *Westminster Review*, in noticing Lingard's *Vindication*, commented, "A history of England by a Roman Catholic priest was assuredly destined to be met with coldness and suspicion. . . . We are disposed to entertain the highest regard for the industry, fidelity, and acuteness of Dr. Lingard."[6] Nor did the *Dublin Review*, under the editorship of Wiseman, probe into Lingard's motives as an historian, although it praised him as "calm, good-tempered, and deliberative."[7] Surely only by their silence, by their failure explicitly to accuse Lingard of having other apologetic motives can such contemporary critics be said to view the historian as a disinterested scholar whose "object is truth." Among Lingard's more recent critics evidence for this view of his motives is similarly scarce.

ii. The Subtle Apologist

In commenting on the reviews of his first three volumes in a letter to his fellow priest, John Kirk, Lingard made what was his clearest, least qualified private statement of his purpose and working criterion: "Whatever I have said or purposely omitted has been through the motive of serving religion."[8] Although seldom so frank and explicit, Lingard's statements professing or admitting, as the case might be, an ultimately pragmatic motive in writing history are plentiful.

For example, he decided against continuing his *Anglo-Saxon Church* into Norman times because "there would be more to disedify than to edify in such a continuation," and this, obviously, would scarcely accord with his view of history as an apologetical

---

5. Cf. below, chapter V.
6. "A Vindication of Certain Passages in His Fourth and Fifth Volumes of the History of England by Dr. Lingard," *Westminster Review*, VII (1827), p. 187.
7. "Dr. Lingard's History of England," *Dublin Review*, XII (May, 1842), p. 312.
8. MS., to John Kirk, December 18, 1819.

weapon, however well concealed. He was personally shocked by the evidence in Wilkin's *Concilia* of monastic scandals.[9] In soliciting and selecting transcripts of documents Lingard had a similar criterion; writing to Robert Gradwell in Rome he said,

> In a word you see what I want—whatsoever may serve to make the Catholic cause appear respectable in the eyes of a British public. I have the reputation of impartiality—therefore have it more in my power to do so.[10]

The previous year the historian had written to Gradwell concerning his new *History*:

> I have written in a different manner from that observed in the *Anglo-Saxon Church*. I have been careful to defend the catholics, but not so as to hurt the feelings of the protestants. Indeed my object has been to write such a work, if possible, as should be read by protestants: under the idea, that the more it is read by them, the less Hume will be in vogue, and consequently the fewer prejudices against us will be imbibed from him.[11]

To avoid all appearance of controversy—that was Lingard's aim in the first edition of his *History*. He saw no point in continuing to write for a small, isolated Catholic audience and by overt controversy make that isolation all the greater. However, towards the end of his life, Lingard admitted that although he had been extremely cautious in 1819, now that he was accepted as a moderate, perhaps impartial writer, he had become bolder by introducing material on the penal law that he had purposely omitted from earlier editions.[12] He had followed the advice he gave to his friend John Walker, to make his first book as perfect as possible, "Like a young girl, you are now coming out, and must therefore appear in your best dress. Later you may be occasionally in deshabille."[13]

Lingard was very much aware of the necessity of accuracy and

---

9. MS., to John Kirk, November 25, 1820.
10. MS., to Robert Gradwell, May 17, 1820.
11. MS., to Robert Gradwell, June 3, 1819.
12. MS., to Edward Price, February 13, 1847.
13. MS., to John Walker, probably December, 1838.

apparent neutrality if he was to accomplish his longer purpose. This apologetic motive underlay even what seemed to his Catholic critics weak, indeed dangerous, concessions to Protestant claims.

That Lingard wrote history for an apologetic purpose resulted partially from his conviction that factual truth alone, once known, was sufficient to remove prejudices and prepare for conversions. Whether this over-confidence in human rationality is evidence of the influence of the waning Enlightenment in which he had spent his youth or of the Benthamism so prevalent in contemporary England is an interesting speculation. In 1840 he wrote to Bishop George Oliver,

> You must silently operate on the prejudices of your Protestant readers. For my own part, I conceive that he who contributes to remove prejudices now, lays the groundwork of conversions hereafter; for prejudice in general indisposes Protestants, not only from yielding to argument, but even from listening to it.[14]

With this conviction was another: that books which non-Catholics would read, rather than controversial pamphlets or replies to critics, were the truly beneficial apologetic weapons. Walker, the publisher of Lingard's tracts against the Anglican Bishop of Durham, had asked the historian in 1813, "After all, what is the use of these pamphlets? Few Protestants will read them. If you wish to make an impression, write books that Protestants will read."[15] "This," he afterwards said, "led to the composition of the *History*."[16] For even though Lingard's two chief works created controversies among Catholics, they caused no less interest among Protestants. And this was his object.

Even though Dr. Lingard's histories were widely read, his subtle motives did not escape all of his critics. The *Quarterly Review* and the *Edinburgh Review* on several occasions acknow-

---

14. November 9, 1840, quoted in Tierney, "Memoir," p. 20.
15. Quoted in Joseph Gillow, ed., *Biographical Dictionary of the English Catholics from the Breach with Rome in 1534 to the Present Time* (London, 1888), IV, p. 259.
16. *Ibid.*

ledged not only his "great care and skill, his scrupulous exactness," but their frustration in being unable to reply to "a bold and regular attack."[17] Henry Hallam, who spoke of Lingard as an author who could not "repress the inveterate partiality of his profession,"[18] agreed with Allen and Southey that the *History of England* was a cleverly fashioned weapon in the hands of a Catholic priest. However, the early nineteenth century was far removed from ages when truth was sought for its own worth; rather, it was the heyday of whig history. Hence we can scarcely expect contemporary critics to discern and appreciate disinterested history, even if they were unexpectedly to find it.

A preliminary conclusion may surely go at least this far: John Lingard's historical writings, although impartial in appearance and approach, were scarcely so in motive and aim. Though "truth" might well have been his object, it was not a disinterested historical truth, sought for its own sake. To facilitate a change of mind in the English people he devoted the scholarly labors of a long life. He saw prejudice as essentially a matter of the mind, not will: facts would do their own work. This learned man retained almost the naïve faith of the Enlightenment that knowledge alone would dissipate bias.

Yet another fertile source of evidence contributing to Lingard's portrait as an apologist in motive lies in his characteristic manner of approach, in his methods, his tone. Throughout his life, and especially during its last decade, when Nicholas Wiseman and the Oxford converts were urging a return to the more external Catholic practices, Lingard counselled caution: Catholics should insist only on the essentials of the faith; the "foreign" practices and devotions would only drive away converts. He "could not believe any human being in England" either sprinkling the congregation with holy water or carrying the cross in procession. Only Protestant ridicule and even public rows would result. The rector of Hornby feared the Protestant reaction to the selection by the new Catholic bishop of the Northern District of the feast of St. Bartholomew for his

---

17. "Lingard's History of England, Volumes 3 and 4," *Quarterly Review*, XXXIII (1825), pp. 5-6.
18. Henry Hallam, quoted in Lingard, *History of England*, 5th ed., I, p. iv.

consecration date. In the same letter he expressed his regret over the publicity being given to a rescript from Rome concerning indulgences, since there was nothing more misunderstood and more objectionable to English Protestants.[19]

As a criterion for writing, Lingard's conciliatory approach was no less marked. Only four years before his death he cautioned against a proposed history of the Catholic penal laws on the ground that it might prompt a new edition of Foxe's *Martyrs* to replay the Marian persecutions.[20] Lingard remained consistently reluctant to reissue any of the small Catholic tracts and pamphlets that he had written as a young man, preferring not to injure his carefully built neutral reputation.[21] In 1840, Lingard wrote his widely read *Catechetical Instructions on the Doctrine and Worship of the Catholic Church*; even in this professedly religious tract, his object was to "make a book which would not scare Protestants at first sight."[22] When his publisher, Joseph Mawman, asked him to suggest topics in his *History* for use in advertisements, Lingard characteristically omitted any that smacked of religious controversy; rather, he suggested the capture of Richard II, the battle of Agincourt, and the murder of Edward II.[23]

No instance of Lingard's apologetic presentation in his *History of England* is better known than his deliberate omission of the source of his documents when he treated the relations of King John and the papal legate Pandulf, a matter still of considerable interest in nineteenth century England.[24]

> It is true . . . that I might originally have made the matter more clear by stating where I had found the charter: but I did not do that then. Why? Because it was an experiment. I was beginning my career as historian of England. I knew the prejudices marshalled against me, and I was afraid that if I had said that I found it in the

19. MS., to John Walker, May, 1841.
20. MS., to Edward Price, January 10, 1847.
21. MS., to Joseph Mawman, July 15, 1823.
22. MS., to John Walker, December 21, 1839.
23. MS., to Joseph Mawman, November 15, 1819.
24. Lingard, *History of England*, 5th ed., III, p. 32.

Vatican, it would immediately have been proclaimed a fraud, etc., etc.[25]

Feeling, however, that he had "secured the reputation of impartiality," as we have seen, Lingard included the reference in his later editions.

His treatment of Thomas a Becket similarly shows that Lingard's concern was to produce a history of England that Protestants would read. This Catholic historian stated simply that, "Thomas Becket was a personage . . . who, since his death, has been alternately portrayed as a saint and hero, or as a hypocrite and traitor, according to the religious bias of the historian."[26] That Lingard later praised the archbishop's defense of the rights of the Church did not prevent Bishop Milner from pointing out that in all Lingard's works he gave the title of "saint" to the martyr of Canterbury only once.

Joan of Arc emerged even less a saint from Lingard's pages: "It is plain that the enthusiast mistook for realities the workings of her own imagination. . . . An impartial observer would have pitied and respected the mental delusion with which she was afflicted."[27] This surely is an apologetic portrait of a saint in an age deploring miracles. Similarly, in his *Anglo-Saxon Church*, Lingard had passed over the famous and controversial miracles of St. Dunstan.[28]

Lingard, only after having dealt quite severely with Catholic Mary, allowed himself to say of Elizabeth:

> To her first parliament she had expressed a wish that on her tomb might be inscribed the title of "the virgin queen." But the woman who despises the safeguards, must be content to forfeit the reputation, of chastity.[29]

This unusual sarcasm, overly mild though it was to many Catholics, brought a worried warning from Mawman, Lingard's publisher.

---

25. MS., to John Coulston, 1834.
26. Lingard, *History of England*, 5th ed., II, p. 197.
27. *Ibid.*, V, pp. 78, 90.
28. Lingard, *Anglo-Saxon Church*, 2nd ed., II, p. 319.
29. Lingard, *History of England*, 5th ed., VIII, p. 144.

The historian replied that he "should be sorry to say anything that may hurt the sale of the book," and offered to change "any expression."[30] Again to avoid what was to him unnecessary controversy, Lingard was willing neither to include a discussion of the general results of the reformation nor to continue his *History* into the Glorious Revolution. The latter, he felt, was held in such universal whig esteem that any even implicit criticism would only harm the *History*'s acceptance.[31]

Lingard's apologetic moderation showed not only in the presentation of his own historical works, but also in his manner of refuting the errors and criticisms of his contemporaries. That Dr. Lingard was free from "angry expression, arrogance, and indignation," and showed only a "placid indifference" even one of his most vigorous opponents, John Allen of the *Edinburgh Review*, admitted.[32] Yet it was Allen who six years previously had made what was perhaps the most violent attack on Lingard, when the latter had, in a note in the fifth volume of the History, described the St. Bartholomew's massacre as a spontaneous, unpremeditated rising. Indeed, so unusually hostile was Allen's review that Lingard, contrary to his custom, determined to reply. This he did, "effectually but genteely," in his meticulously researched *Vindication of Certain Passages in the Fourth and Fifth Volumes of the History of England;* the source analysis in this tract showed Lingard at his critical best.[33] His restraint, indeed, under the circumstances, allowed him to write to Mawman, "Perhaps I have not been so severe as you would wish, but I think I hurt his feelings more by treating his abuse with a tone of contempt. It will appear more dignified; and he will not have the pleasure of asserting that he has vexed me."[34]

Although Lingard had only the deepest contempt for the historical accuracy and acumen of his two famous contemporaries,

---

30. MS., to Joseph Mawman, 1823.
31. MS., to John Kirk, December 18, 1819; only afterwards did Lingard's general acceptance persuade him to continue to 1689.
32. John Allen, "Lingard's History of England," *Edinburgh Review*, LIII (March. 1831), p. 19.
33. Cf. below, chapter IV.
34. MS., to Joseph Mawman, December, 1826.

Macaulay and Carlyle, and had made an extensive list of the former's errors, he refrained from publishing them. This, he felt, would come better from a non-Catholic. In the quiet seclusion of Hornby, Lingard became increasingly convinced of the futility of overt aggressiveness; what there was of this quality in his *Anglo-Saxon Church* had only served to involve him in a long controversy with the Anglican bishop of Durham.

That this life-long habit of restraint in his published writings for the sake of his apologetic motive did not always come easy is evident from the contrast which his private correspondence affords: it fairly brims at times with caustic contempt and ridicule. While he restricted his published comments on Lord Macaulay to a very few documented footnotes, he privately expressed his contempt:

> One half of the quotations from him are of no authority. He has been fishing in cesspools and quagmires, and has filled his memory with all kinds of filth and falsehood, which he retails, mixed up with facts, as if they were facts also. You might as well believe all the skits and witticism and falsehoods which are prevalent during a contested election. . . . His work abounds in claptrap of every description.[35]

The burden of evidence, contemporary and more recent, can leave little doubt concerning the question: what was the impelling motive for John Lingard the historian? He was, by conscious choice, throughout his life, an apologist. But that should cause no chagrin or surprise: for he was, after all, a missionary of Douai. The "truth" that he set as his goal was truth for a still more ultimate purpose. He searched for past truth to justify and explain and make acceptable the cause of his Church in both past and present England. His goal was a pragmatic truth, but still truth. His motive did not detract from the soundness and veracity of the facts he presented.

---

35. MS., to John Walker, December 27, 1848.

iii. A whig Historian?

Closely interwoven with the problem of Lingard's motive is his relation to what has been called the whig school of history. It is with this group, dominant, as we have seen, in his generation, that he is most usually classified by modern surveys of historiography. To determine whether the appellation "whig historian" may be justly applied to Dr. Lingard we shall examine the evidence of his own and contemporary estimates.

What were his own political preferences or allegiances? We should in this connection recall the general political complexion of the "Hornby circle," and indeed, of all of Lingard's known associates: they were in great majority Whig in politics. Privately he rejoiced at the Whig parliamentary victory in 1830, and the appointments of Earl Grey as Prime Minister and Lord Brougham as Chancellor.[36] Among the historian's few comments on politics, there is a brief facetious message to Wiseman, who was about to depart for Rome, "Tell Pope Gregory that as long as he adheres to Peel and Wellington, he will receive no more veneration from me than I owe him as head of the church."[37] But in the 1830's Catholic Tories were few, for it was the party of Wellington and Peel which had so long postponed emancipation. Yet the political whiggism of Lingard was a far cry from that of Macaulay. Indeed, very probably the rector of Hornby and many of the older Catholics could, on the basis of deeper, longer sympathies, have said with the Whig O'Connell that at heart they were Tories. Surely no thoroughgoing Whig could have written, as Lingard did, in 1848 of the revolution in France, "Yet I entertain a hope that a monarchial government will yet be established."[38]

Whig though he was in his restricted political life, the historian could assure his publisher, ". . . I persuade myself that no writer has hitherto sat down to the task more free from political pre-

---

36. MS., from William Shepherd, December, 1830.
37. MS., to Nicholas Wiseman, January, 1836.
38. MS., to John Walker, February 20, 1848.

possessions than myself."[39] At greater length, in the preface to his sixth volume, he wrote of himself:

> It has been his endeavour to hold with a steady hand the balance between the contending parties, and to delineate with equal fidelity the virtues and the vices of the principal actors, whether they supported the pretensions of the crown, or fought for the liberties of the people. Having no political partialities to gratify, he knows not of any temptation, which was likely in this respect to seduce him from the straight line of his duty.[40]

A second norm, perhaps more proximately important than Lingard's personal political affiliations, in determining the existence or character of his whiggism was his view of the relation of the past to the present. In 1842 the *Dublin Review* made an estimate of Lingard that could scarcely be applied to a simon-pure whig: he was the first of historians to have the "common sense to see the real insignificance, for all modern practical purposes, of all past events." He narrated, for example, the Stuart attempts at religious tolerance on their own merits, not merely as background factors to 1688.

The *North British Review*, though hardly so commendatory, also noticed that this whig principle of history was lacking in Lingard: "In reading his pages, we miss the ardour for popular rights and freedom which lends such a charm to the *Norman Conquest* by Augustin Thierry." Allen commented similarly that, "Dr. Lingard . . . relates, with lifeless coldness, the establishment of Magna Carta, and commemorates the termination of the struggle in the time of Edward I with freezing indifference."[41] In contrast to Macaulay and Hallam, Froude and Freeman, Lingard failed to interpret the reformation as an advance towards freedom; rather, he viewed it as a break in English tradition and continuity.[42]

---

39. MS., to Joseph Mawman, July 12, 1824.
40. Lingard, *History of England* (London, 1825), VI, p. v.
41. John Allen, "Lingard's History of England," *Edinburgh Review*, XLII (1825), p. 6.
42. John Lingard, *A Collection of Tracts on Several Subjects connected with the Civil and Religious Principles of Catholics* (London, 1826), p. 237; cf. below, pp. 85-95.

These contemporary estimates notwithstanding, Lingard wrote in the preface to his first edition:

> The historian ought not confine himself to the barren recital of facts. It is his duty to trace the silent progress of nations from barbarism to refinement; and to mark their successive improvements in the arts of legislation and government. But in the performance of this duty he must keep a steady rein on the imagination; or he will mistake fiction for truth, and write a romance in place of history.[43]

His suggestion to his publisher that annual parliaments and universal suffrage, then so widely discussed on the eve of the first Reform Bill, be advertised as treated in his *History* must be taken more as a selling device than as whiggism.[44] If Lingard was a whig historian on the score of viewing history as the story of freedom, he was such a reticent one that he disappointed his less restrained contemporaries.

In the question of acting as judge or interpreter or philosopher of history this Catholic priest was even less a whig. For nothing did he have greater contempt and distrust than for the "philosophy of history." Already in the preface to his first edition Lingard was explicit: "I have little hesitation in saying, that few writers have done more to pervert the truth of history than philosophical historians."[45] At the very end of his life, for his last edition, he reaffirmed that, "It is long since I disclaimed any pretensions to that which has been called the philosophy of history, but which might with more propriety be termed the philosophy of romance."[46]

In an age of philosophical history, critics ranging from Allen to Wiseman recognized its absence in Lingard's writings. They had, in fact, no choice; factual detail, not general laws, specific events, not moral lessons dominated the *History*: so much so that it was open to the contrary charge of dryness rather than of glittering generality.

---

43. John Lingard, *History of England* (London, 1819), I, p. iv.
44. MS., to Joseph Mawman, November 15, 1819.
45. Written in 1823. Lingard, *History of England*, 5th ed., I, p. xxvii.
46. *Ibid.*, I, p. xxv.

Dr. Lingard was equally critical of his fellow Catholics who tended, as he wrote in 1849, "to form a notion of the design of providence first, and then press every event into the accomplishment of that design."[47] Lingard was unwilling to join Bancroft in seeing and interpreting the hand of God in the specific events of history; those who did he regarded more as pious enthusiasts than as historians. The series in the *Rambler*, "Modern Saints," for which Father Frederick Faber wrote a preface, were characterized by Lingard as "romances."[48] He gave as an instance the sentence, "God raised up the saints Ignatius and Philip Neri to reform the Catholic world, Ignatius to reform the Catholic intellect, Philip to reform the Catholic heart." To Lingard, history must, in method and presentation, if not in motive, be factual and neutral. Reviewing Dodd's *Church History*, he praised its enabling the reader "to distinguish the real facts of history from the slanderous fables of religious sectarianism."[49]

Repeatedly the author of the *Anglo-Saxon Church* and the *History of England* claimed freedom from bias: "I am not conscious to myself of any feeling which should induce me to pervert the truth."[50] In the lengthy preface which he wrote at the age of seventy-eight, the historian recalled that he had constantly ". . . to watch with jealousy the secret workings of my own personal feelings and prepossessions. Such vigilance is a matter of necessity to every writer of history."[51] He must detach himself from the scenes and causes he describes; the unconcerned spectator must be his model.

Although Lingard's critics to an uncommon degree admitted his fairness, he did not wholly escape censure. Allen, for example, accused him of too great devotion to the Church, a charge which indeed would have pleased and reassured Bishop Milner. Later,

---

47. MS., to F. C. Husenbeth, March 19, 1849.
48. *Ibid.*
49. John Lingard, "Dodd's Church History of England," *Dublin Review*, VI (1839), pp. 402-403.
50. Written in 1823. Lingard, *History of England*, 5th ed., I, p. xxix.
51. *Ibid.*, I, p. xii.

Allen admitted that Lingard had "corrected the too usual tendency to introduce a party spirit in the historical narrative."[52]

If John Lingard is to be classed as a whig historian, it must be only with qualifications, and more, perhaps, because of his motive than because of his working principles. He wrote for a pragmatic purpose, but in a strikingly unpragmatic way. He studied the past to help convert the present, but in narrating that past did not pervert it with his personal philosophy and judgments. He was not the disinterested scholar, but still he respected the historical fact. He narrated history, but he did not, as a true whig historian must, presume to discern and reveal its "laws" or the laws of its providence. If John Lingard was a whig historian, he was so in purpose, not in product.

---

52. John Allen, "Lingard's History of England," *Edinburgh Review*, XLII (April, 1825), p. 22.

CHAPTER IV

METHOD: TO THE FOUNTAINHEAD

The last chapter was concerned with Lingard's motive, this with his method. There we attempted to answer the question, why did he write history? Here, how did he write it? Dr. Lingard's admittedly apologetic purpose has accounted, perhaps more than any other factor, for his position in historiography being so commonly questioned, or better, ignored. In contrast, his historical method constitutes his strongest claim to a significant place in the development of historical writing. It is on the basis of his method that Lingard has been granted, at least by some, a unique position in English historiography.

"He was the founder of an historical school, the school of scientific history," is one recent estimate.[1] Another views Lingard's *History* as the first English historical work based directly on primary sources.[2] Still another reminds us that to demand original sources a hundred and fifty years ago was itself original.[3] Philip Hughes goes so far as to say that in the use of sources, "Lingard is easily the superior of most historians of our own time."[4]

John Lingard's method need not be merely inferred from his writings; it was the result of conscious effort. In the preface to the first edition of his *History of England*, he wrote.

> In composing it I have faithfully adhered to the rule, which I prescribed to myself in the preceding volumes; to take nothing upon credit, to distrust the statements of partial and interested writers, and to consult every authen-

---

1. W. J. Hegarty, "Lingard Centenary," *Irish Ecclesiastical Record*, 5th ser., LXXVI (November, 1951), p. 392.
2. Gerard Culkin, "Making Lingard's History," *Month*, n.s., VI (July, 1951), p. 7.
3. Christopher Hollis, "Lingard," *Historical Bulletin*, XI (March, 1933), p. 43.
4. Philip Hughes, "Centenary Tribute," *History Today*, I (April, 1951), p. 58.

tic document within my reach. Fidelity and research are
the indispensable duties of the Historian.[5]

In 1806 he had already advanced his famous questions: ". . . in the
pursuit of truth I have made it a religious duty to consult the
original historians. Who would draw from the troubled stream,
when he may drink at the fountain-head?"[6]

i. Sources

The famous controversy between Lingard and John Allen
concerning the St. Bartholomew Massacre gave rise to many of
the former's explicit, discriminating descriptions of his sources.
In the first edition of his *History*, Lingard said that he had consulted "the most authentic documents" concerning the massacre;[7]
Allen, in his review, changed the wording to, "the most original
documents."[8] This prompted Lingard in his *Vindication* to draw
clearly the distinction that is now so intrinsic to historical method:
the difference between the authenticity and the credibility of an
historical source. The mere temporal originality of a document,
though itself an improvement over an obviously later, secondary
account, must not be equated with the believability or reliability
of that source's contents. Lingard asked directly: how did the
document's author get his information—as an eyewitness or in-
directly; was he of credible character? Already, then, in 1826,
Lingard clearly distinguished internal from external criticism in
his evaluation and use of documents.[9] Only our terminology has
changed: what he called "original," is now commonly "authentic";
when he spoke of "authentic," we employ "credible."

In this same defense, Dr. Lingard drew a distinction between
public and private documents as historical sources, in an age, when,
on the one hand, Macaulay was largely ignoring the former, and

---

5. Lingard, *History of England* (London, 1819), IV, p. v.
6. Lingard, *Anglo-Saxon Church* (Newcastle, 1806), I, p. vi.
7. Lingard, *History of England* (London, 1819), IV, p. v.
8. Allen, "Lingard's History of England," *Edinburgh Review*, XLIV (June, 1826),
   p. 94.
9. John Lingard, *A Vindication of Certain Passages in the Fourth and Fifth
   Volumes of the History of England*, 2nd ed. (London, 1826), pp. 10-11.

Ranke, in contrast, the latter. Lingard gave critical credence to both:

> A broad distinction should be drawn between authority for a public fact, and authority for a secret design. . . . . Its [a secret design] existence can be shown only by the confession of the parties, or by the testimony of those, who have derived their knowledge from these parties. Such confession or testimony would be authority, and contemporary authority.[10]

Lingard prefaced the opening volume of his *History of England* with what was in 1819 a unique claim, "The author has spared no pains in consulting the most ancient historians and comparing their narratives with such authentic documents as are known to exist."[11] The degree to which Lingard achieved his novel objective may be gauged from the comment of his most searching critic: "He possesses what he claims, the rare merit of having collected his materials from original records. . . . To borrow his own metaphor, he has not drunk from the troubled stream, but drank from the fountainhead."[12]

Lingard was aware, as Allen indicated, not only of the value of genuine and credible sources, but also of the dangers and short-comings of secondary accounts. That he appreciated these correlative critical principles he showed already in 1819; in composing the first volumes of his *History* he had not only sought out the "original and authentic writers" but purposely refrained from reading the modern or secondary accounts. For example, he specifically claimed that in the previous eight years he had not read "a

---

10. *Ibid.*, pp. 21-22.
11. Lingard, *History of England* (London, 1819), I, p. iii. As an instance of his primary citations, cf. this note which he appended to his treatment of King Alfred in his 5th edition: "For Alfred, see Heming. Chart. i, 42; Asser., i, 3; for Edward, Gale, iii, p. 362; for Athelstan, id., p. 364. The coins in Camden, Tab. 4, 5, in Hick's Diss. tab. ii, and the MS. In the Cotton library, Tiberius, A.2. Athelstan ab omnibus imperator totius Britanniae est pronuntiatus. Flor. 693, Subactis ubique hostibus totius Britanniae dominium obtinuit. Sim. Dun. 18. He calls himself Rex totius Britanniae. . . . Cod. Dip. ii, 183, 194, 208." I, p. 202, note.
12. Allen, "Lingard's History of England," *Edinburgh Review*, XLII, (April, 1825), p. 2.

hundred pages" of Hume that he might not unconsciously "imbibe the prejudices or copy the mistakes of others."[13] Repeatedly Lingard exclaimed, "How many statements . . . in modern histories have no foundation in fact, but are . . . simply repeated by writer after writer."[14]

Introducing his volumes on the controversial sixteenth century, Lingard explained, "Where the ancient authorities are silent, I have preferred to leave the reader to the exercise of his own judgment, than to palm upon him my own conjectures for real facts."[15] But avoiding secondary accounts is not enough:

> It becomes necessary for the writer to point out the sources from which he derives his own information, to fortify his own narrative with quotations from ancient documents, and to show that the contrary statement is not consistent with the original authorities.[16]

Encouraging Dr. Gradwell to search further in the Vatican Library for the original letters of Henry VIII to Anne Boleyn, Lingard said directly, "I know not how these things can be ascertained unless it be from original papers."[17]

The best example of Lingard's working awareness of the essential difference between primary and secondary evidence is his entire *History of England;* it was constructed on this distinction, novel in his day. And as an error perpetuated by successive uncritical historians, he pointed to the last testament of Henry VIII, which, contrary to popular accounts, had never been personally signed by the king.[18]

Lingard was similarly skeptical of national heroes whose luster was the product more of uncritical tradition than of authentic documents. He was accused, for example, of bias against the Scots for tempering his praise of Wallace; in defense he said merely that, "If this be his offense, he [Lingard] pleads guilty, and trusts that

---

13. MS., to Joseph Mawman, November 23, 1820.
14. Lingard, *History of England*, 5th ed., I, p. xxiv.
15. Lingard, *History of England* (London, 1823), IV, p. vi.
16. Lingard, *Anglo-Saxon Church*, 2nd ed., I, p. vii.
17. MS., to Robert Gradwell, June 4, 1819.
18. Lingard, *History of England*, 5th ed., I, p. xviii; and IV, p. 364.

the reader will commend him for having dared to separate the truths of history from the tales of fiction."[19]

The novelty in his day of Lingard's critical view of sources may be seen in the chaotic and neglected state in which they were found. The primary documents of English and European history were still largely in manuscript, often inaccessible and unwanted. Especially little had been done in the field of English historical sources since the sixteenth century. Yet it was here that Lingard did his most original work. Dr. Gradwell reported from Rome that when he came to the English College, he found "a great cartload of dusty and rotting papers on the library floor . . . letters of Cardinal Pole, things in the handwriting of Father Parsons, Garnet, etc."[20] Even the Vatican archives were "jumbled and purloined"—effects of their having been taken to Paris by Napoleon.[21]

Dr. Lingard's distrust of secondary writers, coupled with the disorganized condition of primary sources, did not deter him in his search for materials. As early as 1803, while working on his first volumes of history, he began his system of "research by correspondence," on which he relied throughout the rest of his life. Reverend Joseph Curr, in answer to a series of questions, sent Lingard a quantity of information gathered in the great library which Humphrey Chatham founded in Manchester in 1656.[22] Also, Joseph Hodgson, the former vice-president of Douai, and then in London, described his painstaking efforts to decipher and transcribe the crumbled pages of a "thick vellum MS. in the British Museum, said to have been written in 703, and to have belonged to King Athelstan."[23]

During Lingard's first decade at Hornby, he made many journeys to the Chatham library in Manchester and other private libraries in Liverpool. At this time, too, he received both books and offers of money from the Duke of Norfolk and Edward Blount, Mawman's friend. Thomas Grenville, from his library of

19. *Ibid.*, III, p. 241.
20. MS., from Robert Gradwell, July 31, 1819.
21. MS., from Robert Gradwell, March 22, 1821.
22. Haile and Bonney, *Life and Letters*, p. 85.
23. *Ibid.*

some 20,000 volumes, supplied the *History of Persecutions of the Church of Scotland*, for which Lingard had been looking. He received information from the library at Stonyhurst, even though his relations with the Jesuits were for a time less than cordial because Father Plowden suspected him of Gallicanism:

> They have spontaneously furnished me with several scarce books; among others with the MS. account of the Gunpowder Plot in English, in the very handwriting of Father Gerard. You [Gradwell] sent me from Rome the Italian translation in MS. The English MS. is perpetually corrected by another hand, and the Italian comprehends in the corrections.[24]

For his fifth edition, in which he incorporated much new material, Sir Robert Peel procured for Lingard copies of documents in the State Paper Office relating to the Gunpowder Plot.[25] Lord Lansdowne, too, permitted the historian to inspect the family archives.[26]

Lingard carried his personal search for sources to the continent during his two visits in 1817 and 1825. During the first trip he kept a journal, which though largely a travelogue, contained many historical references. For example, he recorded his visit to Sens in France:

> May 3rd.—The foundations of the walls of Sens still remain of Roman architecture. The stones are much larger than any I ever saw used in England. . . . I visited its Cathedral, a Gothic building not unhandsome. It preserves many antiques. It was here St. Thomas of Canterbury met Alexander III. In a chapel dedicated to him is a painting of their interview. I put on his chasuble, to show the ladies the form it bore anciently. . . .[27]

Lingard's purpose in going to Rome was to consult sources in the Vatican Library before publishing his first volumes. Although

24. MS., to Robert Gradwell, April, 1822.
25. Thomas P. Peardon, *The Transition in English Historical Writing* (New York, 1933), p. 282; and MS., to Nicholas Sewall, S.J., December 7, 1821.
26. MSS., to Joseph Mawman, September 1, 1822; and to George Oliver, August 11, 1827.
27. Quoted in Haile and Bonney, *Life and Letters*, p. 141.

Cardinal Litta, the Prefect of the Propaganda, then in charge of the Church in England, was cool and distrustful to his requests, as a result of Bishop Milner's warning, the Papal Secretary of State, the famous Cardinal Consalvi, ordered the Vatican librarian to comply with all of Dr. Lingard's requests for manuscripts.[28]

The Vatican archives in 1817 were still in great confusion and in large part yet unpacked since their return from Paris, where Napoleon had taken them. Lingard, however, was particularly happy, because of Protestant interest in the question, to find the register of Innocent III relating to Pandulf's legation and King John. His researches took him also to the Ambrosian Library in Milan, and although the Venetian archives were not open until the work of Rawdon Brown, Lingard found in other libraries, especially the Vatican, several dispatches of the Venetian ambassadors. Hence, at least in this limited manner, he antedated Ranke, to whom the first use of these documents is generally attributed.

However, in the seclusion of Hornby, from which he seldom departed, Lingard depended for most of his source materials on his many scholarly correspondents throughout England and especially on the continent. Already at Ushaw, he made many of the associations later so useful as correspondents willing to transcribe documents for him. Then the success of the first volumes brought him still wider connections, with offers of help in the loan of books and the copying of manuscripts. The historian's most faithful, persevering correspondents included Charles Butler and W. B. Turnbull in London, Robert Gradwell and Nicholas Wiseman in Rome, and Alexander Cameron, the rector of the English College at Valladolid.[29]

Robert Gradwell, the rector of the newly-restored English College at Rome, and formerly rector at Claughton, not far from Hornby, was Lingard's most fruitful collaborator for over a decade. He personally searched through the leading libraries and archives of Rome: the Vatican, the College of Propaganda, the

---

28. MS., to Joseph Mawman, August 29, 1817.
29. MSS., from Robert Gradwell, April 24, 1824, and August 1, 1818; to Bishop William Poynter, December 12, 1825; also R. L. Smith, "Lingard at Hornby," *Clergy Review*, XXXV (May, 1951), p. 296.

Holy Office, the private collections of the Barbarini and Piombini families, and that of St. Isadore's, the Irish Franciscan house, where he found much on Cromwell's government of Ireland. He also introduced Lingard to the work of Italian historians, to which Gradwell added his own critical comments.

Shortly after Lingard's first return from Rome, Gradwell was able to report that he had, "A more ample license and better means of getting these instruments copied than any Englishman ever had."[30] For £150 he could get transcribed everything yet unpublished in the Vatican concerning England. He made special reference to the warning of Monsignor Marini, the Vatican archivist, that many previously made transcriptions of papal letters and bulls were full of interpolations and omissions. Lingard, though dependent and grateful for the manuscript transcriptions, repeatedly worried, "Who is to make the selection? . . . I fear an immense mass of papers will be found."[31] The future Cardinal Wiseman, the next rector of the English College, continued Gradwell's research and obtained transcripts for Lingard. Through his Roman correspondents, then, for thirty years following 1817, Lingard obtained enormous collections of copies of papal letters, correspondence of the papal agents in seventeenth century England, Con, Panzani, Rossetti, and D'Adda; letters of Mary, Queen of Scots, as well as reports of the Venetian ambassadors in the Barbarini archives of the reign of Elizabeth.

Lingard's Spanish correspondents were less successful. Alexander Cameron described the handicaps under which he attempted to gather materials for Lingard at Valladolid. The archivist never allowed Cameron to see the documents, but insisted on merely reading them rapidly to him, during which he could take no notes. Only later could he write from memory what he had heard. Although Cameron's successor, Thomas Sherborne, fared a little better, this source was never satisfactory to Lingard. Hence, he never used materials from Valladolid unless they were elsewhere confirmed, nor was he able to cite exact pages in his references to the records found in Simancas.

---

30. MS., from Robert Gradwell, August 1, 1818.
31. MS., to Robert Gradwell, September 24, 1818.

Likewise unavailing were Lingard's efforts to obtain manuscripts relative to the Babington plot, which he had been told by several naval officers were in the archives at Malta. Through Bishop Poynter he applied to the bishop of Malta from transcripts. But even after a careful search, none could be found. Though unsuccessful, Lingard's efforts to obtain these documents shows his scholarly diligence.

Dr. Lingard's constant efforts to keep abreast of new discoveries and publications of historical sources was just as impressive as his initial research. In preparing his *Vindication* he used Chateaubriand's *Les mélanges littéraires* for the Vatican archival sources it contained, which Chateaubriand had read when the Vatican papers were in Paris. The fact that the French work appeared only in the same year as Lingard's *Vindication* shows the rapidity with which he utilized new continental sources.

Reviewing Tierney's revision of Dodd's *Church History*, Lingard commended individual and governmental interest and subsidies in making available an increasing number of historical sources.[32] In 1842 he began revising his *Antiquities of the Anglo-Saxon Church*. "It will be long, however, I fear, before it goes to press," he wrote to Bishop Oliver, "for I am resolved to examine very narrowly before I publish . . . and have rewritten all for the sake of the notes."[33]

The most impressive evidence of Lingard's awareness of the latest historical discoveries and publications was contained in his last revision of the *History of England*. His long preface was, in substance, a critical historiographical essay covering the developments during the thirty years since his first edition:

Since the year 1819, in which the first portion of this work was sent to the press, many new sources of information have been opened to the writer of English history. From time to time, ancient documents of high interest and indisputable authority have been rescued from oblivion, by searches made under the auspices of the Record

---

32. John Lingard, "Dodd's Church History of England," *Dublin Review*, VI (1839), p. 409.
33. MS., to George Oliver, May 3, 1842.

Commission, or through the zeal and enterprise of literary societies and private individuals. It has been my endeavor to embody the substance of all such discoveries in this present library edition . . . by interweaving the new matter with the old in one continuous narrative throughout the work.[34]

The aged historian proceeded then to discuss discriminatingly more than twenty major historical works. In the Anglo-Saxon period Lingard singled out for favorable notice Petrie's *Corpus Historicum*, Benjamin Thorpe's *Ancient Laws and Institutes of England*, and *Homilies of Aelfric*, and John M. Kemble's *Codex Diplomaticus Aevi Saxonici*. As worthy contributions to the history of medieval England, Lingard discussed the *Patres Ecclesiae Anglicanae* of Giles, of particular value for the documents regarding Henry II and St. Thomas of Canterbury.[35] Lingard singled out as particularly valuable source additions both the *Close* and *Patent Rolls*, edited under the Record Commission, and Palgrave's *Parliamentary Writs*. Edited, printed primary documents of this caliber had simply been unavailable when Lingard had written his earlier editions.

The sixteenth century was especially enriched by recent publications. At length Lingard described the *State Papers* of Henry VIII, Sharpe's *Memorials of the Rebellion of 1569*, the *Recueil des Lettres de Marie Stuart*, edited by Labanoff, the Bowes and Leiscester correspondence, as well as the Landsdowne and Harleian collections. Of particular interest and use to Lingard were the *Dépêches* of Fenelon, the French ambassador to Elizabeth's court after 1568, which were edited by Charles Cooper, secretary of the Record Commission.

In his notice of Carlyle's *Letters and Speeches of Oliver Cromwell*, Lingard drew a necessary distinction:

> . . . These documents are well worth the serious attention
> of the historical student. I mean the letters and speeches

---

34. Lingard, *History of England*, 5th ed., I, p. ix.
35. Here, interestingly, Lingard used the title, "saint," now that he had "won acceptance," *ibid.*

themselves, not the running commentary with which the editor accompanied them, in language most glowing and oracular.

Lingard's estimate, however, that Cromwell's works were "collected and published with great care and accuracy" can no longer be accepted.[36] Also among the new seventeenth century publications Lingard noted the *Histoire de la Révolution de 1688, en Angleterre,* by Mazure, who, at his death, deeded his voluminous manuscripts to the historian at Hornby. Finally, Lingard commended Agnes Strickland for utilizing private journals and diaries as historical sources in her *Lives of the Queens of England.*

Dr. Lingard concluded this significant critical essay by stressing the particular value of private documents:

> Among these sources of historical information there is one, which deserves his peculiar attention; the confidential correspondence of persons in high and official situations. This offers him the most valuable assistance. It removes the veil which policy has drawn before the counsels of princes, reveals the secret springs which set in motion the machinery of government, and exhibits kings and ministers in their true characters, not as they affect to appear to the public eye, but as they really were in the privacy of their houses, and in the circle of familiar acquaintances. Without such documents history is an inert and spiritless mass; from these it may drive both vigor and life.[37]

Even before the appearance of the fifth edition of the *History,* Lingard's critics recognized his constant incorporation of the newest historical finds. Allen, for example, commended Lingard's use of hitherto unused, partially unpublished sources concerning the escape of Charles II from the field of Worcester.

---

36. Cf., e.g., Gooch, *History and Historians,* p. 307: "He [Carlyle] made little effort to seek the best text, allowed himself a wide licence in emendations, and modernized the speeches."
37. Lingard, *History of England,* 5th ed., I, p. xxvi.

ii. Criticism

Just as Lingard's concern for primary or original sources was novel in his day, so too was his critical view of them. For example, concerning the common, indeed unanimous, opinion that the St. Bartholomew massacre was planned, Lingard asked,

> But what was their authority? Nothing beyond suspicion, and report, and conjecture. Not one of them, so far as I could discover, pretended to have been privy to the design; not one received his information from those who were supposed to have been privy to it.[38]

He was likewise skeptical of the generally accepted view that France and Spain had concluded, prior to the massacre, a political treaty at Bayonne, designed to destroy the French Huguenots:

> I made it my endeavour to seek out more authentic evidence. In the correspondence of Walsingham, I found a denial on the part of Catharine, that any political business had been transacted at Bayonne: but this I did not mention, because she was interested in the denial. In Strada I discovered the abstract of a letter from Philip of Spain to the archduchess Margaret, who governed the Low Countries, in which the former professed to give to the latter an account of the conferences at Bayonne. . . . If we consider to whom and by whom this letter was written, we must admit it as authentic evidence, and in that case it is most evident that no political treaty was concluded.[39]

Lingard's clear appreciation of the difference between a document's genuineness and its credibility, so essential in modern historical method, is unmistakable here.

Dr. Lingard took nothing on trust. Already in 1820, he was tracking down conflicting texts of Luther's *Epistles* by writing to Oscott College, for he had been "so often misled by quotations."[40]

---

38. Lingard, *Vindication*, p. 20.
39. *Ibid.*, p. 58.
40. MS., to Dr. Weedall, April 13, 1820.

Similarly, he distrusted the published letters of Henry VIII to Anne Boleyn in Hearne's edition of *Avesbury* and Walpole's *Harleian Miscellany*, and asked Gradwell to get him true copies of the originals in the Vatican archives.[41] Lingard's German contemporary, Frederick Raumer, had recently published his *Elizabeth and Mary Queen of Scots*. Lingard caught the "very free translations" and inaccurate use of documents;[42] later John Holmes of the British Museum commended Lingard for his critical evaluation of Raumer's text.

Lingard was particularly anxious to disprove the authenticity of Cardinal Allen's *Admonition to Catholics*, written to be distributed in England at the time of the invasion by the Armada; it attacked Elizabeth as "an incestuous bastard, begotten and born in sin of an infamous courtesan." "After such a publication I am not surprised at anything Elizabeth might do against the catholics."[43] The critical acumen of at least one of Lingard's "research correspondents" appears in Gradwell's reply from Rome:

> . . . The *Admonition* is dated from the "Palace of St. Peter." This can mean nothing else than the Vatican palace . . . but that palace is never called "St. Peter's Palace,". . . the Bullarium shows this. . . . I believe this (simply "The Cardinal") was never the style of a cardinal's signature. I have not yet discovered any reason to suppose that Cardinal Allen ever lived at the Vatican at the time when the *Admonition* was dated.[44]

Lingard's careful criticism was not restricted to the critical sixteenth century. After Allen had attacked the authenticity of a manuscript in the Royal Library in Paris, concerning the captivity of Richard II, Lingard consulted French literary experts, and with their support, defended the document.[45] Letters of Charles II concerning Jacques de la Cloche, his supposed eldest son, furnish

---

41. MS., to Joseph Mawman, September 1, 1822.
42. MS., from John Holmes, February 9, 1838.
43. MS., to Robert Gradwell, September, 1822.
44. MS., from Robert Gradwell, November 18, 1822.
45. John Lingard, "Investigator," *British Press*, IV (October, 1825), p. 450.

another instance of Lingard's closely critical use of documents. He wrote:

> It is impossible to believe that Charles was the writer of the two certificates of birth and of the legacy. 1st. If he had been he would have placed his seal and signature at the top, and not at the bottom. 2nd. He would have written Angleterre, and not Angliterre; he would have known his own title; that Scotland came before France, not after it; that he was Roy d'Irlande, not d'Hybernie, and that he was *défenseur de la foi*, which in no case was to be omitted. 3rd. He would not have said *cacheté du cachet ordinaire noslettres* (there was none such), but *scelle de notre sceau;* he could not have added *sans autre facon et secretariat,* FOR ON SUCH OCCASIONS NO SECRETARY SIGNED. But the title given to the King is sufficient in my mind to prove the fraud—Hybernie is, I suppose, a translation of Hibernia.[46]

This is surely incisive external or textual criticism.

Even the miracles of saints did not escape the historian's criticism. In an anonymous article in the *Catholic Magazine*, Lingard expressed his doubts concerning the famous miracle of St. Januarius.[47] In the same magazine he wrote critically of the tradition behind certain of the expressions in the Litany of Loreto.[48] Ten years earlier, when Dr. Milner asked him to edit the breviary lessons for the English saints, Lingard decided simply to "abridge the original authors; by this means the lessons will be far from elegant, but they will be original."[49]

Lingard's comparison of sources is further evidence of his historical criticism. He justified his following the account of Queen Margaret rather than that of her brother, the duke of Anjou, in determining the hour when Charles gave his consent for the

---

46. MS., to Randall Lythgoe, S.J., March, 1829.
47. John Lingard, "On the Miracles of St. Januarius," *Catholic Magazine*, I (1831), p. 484.
48. John Lingard, "Petitions at Beginnings of Litanies," *Catholic Magazine*, I (1831), p. 546.
49. MS., to John Kirk, October 23, 1821.

massacre on August 24, 1572: "It has always been considered the duty of historians, when the relations, though they agree in substance, disagree in minor circumstances, to prefer that which they think the most probable."

In discussing the crucial question of the relation of the Roman and English churches after the Norman Conquest, he compared Roman and domestic primary accounts.[50] "On many subjects the only sure way of coming at the truth, is to compare together the different letters in the several collections which allude to the same thing."[51] Previously, in reply to Allen's criticism of the *Anglo-Saxon Church*, Lingard cited two ancient and relatively reliable historians: one, a contemporary biographer of Archbishop Dunstan, who signed his manuscript only as "B"; and the other, Eadmer, who wrote about the year 1100. The former document was still extant in the Cotton Library and was published by the Bollandists.[52]

Lingard's estimate and use of non-English sources is evident from what he wrote in 1823: "Even with respect to domestic history, the most authentic and interesting information may often be drawn from the reports made by foreign ambassadors in England to their respective sovereigns."[53] This Lingard was already doing when Leopold von Ranke began, in 1828, to tap the Venetian archives. Hume had based his account of Mary Tudor on the dispatches of the French ambassador, Noailles, printed in Leyden in 1763. From these he had painted the conventional picture of her cruelty, as well as of the supposed Catholic purpose under Gardiner, of handing England over to Spain. Lingard happened on a small book by Henri Griffet, S. J., *Nouveaux éclarissements sur l'histoire de Marie, reine d'Angleterre . . . adressés à M. David Hume*, published in Amsterdam in 1766, which pointed out that in almost every case the French versions were contradicted by the reports of the imperial ambassador, Renard. Although no indication was given of the location of these letters, Lingard, with the help of the

50. Lingard, *History of England* (1825), VI, p. vii.
51. MS., to John Kirk, January, 1821.
52. John Lingard, "A Reply to the Observations of the Edinburgh Review on the Anglo-Saxon Antiquities," *Pamphleteer*, VII (1816), p. 532.
53. Lingard, *History of England*, 5th ed., I, p. xxvi.

archbishop of Paris, found them at Besançon. With them, he was
able to cast Mary, Gardiner, and English Catholics in a wholly
new light.[54] Similarly, his reevaluation of Elizabeth resulted partially from his study of Philip II's papers found at Simancas.

Further evidence of Lingard's critical acumen was his characteristic thoroughness and exactness. Sir A. W. Ward indeed
remarked in 1916 that, "There never was a more vigilant recorder
of facts than Lingard, or one whom criticism was less successful in
convicting of unfounded statements." Examples of Dr. Lingard's
precision abound. His letters of 1839 reveal the minute care with
which he prepared his essay, "When Did Ann Boleyn Leave
France?", which he wrote upon his election to the French Academy. His discovery of the full texts of several of Henry's letters
to Anne allowed Lingard to remark that their language was un-
mistakably that of a man who had only one object: to fulfill an
unlawful passion. In 1847 Lingard was invited to present a window
for a new chapel at Ushaw. He consented, but only on the
condition that it contain the figures of St. Aldhelm, Venerable
Bede, and Alcuin, each attired in his authentic costume. To assure
accuracy, he sent drawings, calling attention to several historical
points: the absence of crosier and mitre, and the exact form of the
chasuble and stole of Aldhelm.[55]

That John Lingard had a marked ability in foreign languages, a
tool necessary in any true historical research, there is no doubt.
He knew latin, Greek, and Hebrew well from his classical training
at Douai. In French he was as fluent as in English, and had a
sufficient knowledge of Spanish and Italian. At the age of sixty he
began to study German in order to read Raumer. Lastly, he also
knew Anglo-Saxon, as a critic testified: "His knowledge of the
Saxon language . . . is very considerable, and the industry of his
research into original authorities is greatly to be commended."[56]
His facility in languages was a valuable research tool; for example,
he was able to revise the accepted account of St. Dunstan's disputed

---

54. *Ibid.*, VII, pp. 110-138; cf. below, pp. 91, 94-95.
55. MS., to Robert Tate, February 6, 1847.
56. "The Antiquities of the Anglo-Saxon Church," *Quarterly Review*, VII (1812),
    p. 105.

role in the tragedy at Calne by relying on the original manuscript of the Saxon Chronicle.[57]

iii. Presentation and Style

On two scores, John Lingard's major work, the *History of England from the First Invasion by the Romans to the Accession of William and Mary in 1688,* must be accounted as quite conventional. His principle of periodization was not trends or movements or ideas, but the reigns of English monarchs in chronological sequence. Only his first volume, which is a somewhat topical treatment of first Roman Britain and then Anglo-Saxon, is an exception. From the Norman Conquest to the Glorious Revolution the conventional and admittedly often artificial organization is determined by kings and queens. "Edward II," "Edward III," and "Richard II" are the chapter titles in the fourteenth century; the enclosure movement, the Black Death, the Hundred Years War, the growth of heresy are made to fit these divisions. It is true, however, that particularly the reformation, although still nominally divided by reigns, Lingard considered as a movement or topic having its own intrinsic unity and cohesion. On the other hand, this arrangement happily preserved the author from a later tendency to see stark divisions between, for example, "medieval" and "modern" England.

On the second account of the internal balance of political, social, economic, or intellectual stress or viewpoint, Dr. Lingard recognized his conscious limitations. "It is complained that I have not mentioned the arts, manners, literature, etc. I will briefly state the reason. I am anxious to finish my work if possible."[58] He went on to explain, even then only half way through, what a long task it had become, and "when a man has passed his fiftieth year he cannot promise himself many years of life or at least of health, and therefore have determined to confine myself to national transactions." To his publisher he responded, "Whether my *History*

---

57. A century later, Eleanor Duckett in her *Saint Dunstan of Canterbury* (New York, 1954), p. 188, substantiates Lingard's view.
58. MS., to John Kirk, November 25, 1820.

will be, as you call it, the *History* of the people, I know not."[59]
It is largely in the tradition of political history—while not so
narrow as to be by any means a mere "drum and trumpet" narrative, still neither was it social history in the mold of John Richard
Green two generations later. The strong thread of interest in the
church and religion in English history prevented the story from
being so wholly political and military as Freeman was to be.

Criticism, both contemporary and recent, of Lingard's style has
been remarkably uniform: never has he been accused of flamboy-
ancy or over-dramatization, qualities surely common to the whig
historians. Indeed, the most frequent and undoubtedly justified
criticism is that his style too completely lacked these elements.
"The most important Revolutions glide before us, without any
anticipation of their approach, notice of their arrival, or retrospective of their effects."[60] There is no better example of this
flatness than Lingard's treatment of the Glorious Revolution: a
purely factual, unembellished narrative. Nothing contrasts more
with Hallam and Macaulay.

Already in 1820, Lingard wrote to John Kirk concerning a
mutual friend's criticism of the first volumes of the *History of
England*,

> I am as much, perhaps, more dissatisfied with the style
> than he is. But style is become with me a secondary
> object. The task I have imposed on myself of taking
> nothing on credit, but of going to the original author, is
> so laborious, that I have no time to throw away on the
> graces of style.[61]

Lingard's somewhat flat style of narration at least in part resulted
from conscious choice. For he was "the unimpassioned narrator
always, stating simply the case before him, allowing the facts to
speak for themselves." This neutral, factual narrative also suited
well Dr. Lingard's apologetical purpose and approach. It reflected
too his opposition to the current philosophical history, drawn

---

59. MS., to Joseph Mawman, July 8(?), 1824.
60. Allen, "Lingard's History of England," *Edinburgh Review*, XLII, p. 2.
61. MS., to John Kirk, December 18, 1820.

necessarily in generous, sweeping lines. No less did his reticent style contrast with both the pious and the pompous in sectarian writing; he thought that the future Cardinal Wiseman, in an article on the apostolic succession, "seemed to be delivering lectures to divinity students."[62]

More positively, Lingard's narrative was consistently clear, his selection and organization of material skillful and judicious. To evaluate rightly his powers of selection and condensation, one must recall the disorganized state in which he found most of his sources and the lack of any reliable guide in constructing a general history of England, for he refused, as we have seen, to use Hume. Often his emphasis was original; his detailed description of the Great Fire and the Plague antedated Macaulay's famous chapters by twenty-five years.

Rarely did Lingard lose his equanimity of expression, born also of his apologetic motive. Seldom did sarcasm or sharpness surface. He avoided expressions at all likely to arouse controversy; when, for example, Mawman pointed out the sectarian overtones of the term "gospellers" as descriptive of the sixteenth century English dissenters, Lingard quickly changed it.[63]

Lingard's contemporaries recognized the novelty and merit of his essentially narrative presentation. John Allen, his most persistent critic, paid him a high compliment: "His diction has the ornament of Gibbon without his affectation and obscurity."[64]

John Lingard's historical method—his discovery and insistence on primary sources, his discriminating criticism of them, his factual presentation—constitutes his most significant contribution to historiography. "In this respect, Lingard is easily the superior of most historians of our own time"—and most assuredly of his own. And of the three classic steps or procedures within historical method, Lingard excelled as an innovator in the first two—heuristic and criticism, while in synthesis he was considerably more conventional.

---

62. MS., to John Walker, n.d.
63. MS., to Joseph Mawman, September, 1822.
64. Allen, "Lingard's History of England," *Edinburgh Review,* XLII, p. 1.

CHAPTER V

LINGARD AND HIS CONTEMPORARIES

How did John Lingard, in view of his motive and his method, appear to his contemporaries, and they to him? Although we have already seen something of the contemporary opinion of him, here we shall consider it in more detail and on its own merits. His works and views were of interest in his own day to his fellow historians and historical critics and to his fellow Catholics. These, then, constitute the two groups whose opinions must be considered.

i. Contemporary Historians and Critics

Although Lingard was only a boy when David Hume died, it was the latter's *History of England* that was still in 1819 the most widely read and generally accepted work on the subject. Hence this eighteenth century Tory historian was for many critics the norm by whom to judge Lingard. The Tory *Quarterly Review*, in commenting on the *Anglo-Saxon Church*, admitted that Hume, in denying that clerical celibacy antedated the tenth century, was corrected by Lingard. "The authority of Bede and the earlier councils are decisive,"[1] the reviewer admitted, and these sources Lingard used. When he came to review this same work, Allen also referred to Hume:

> If a person of note is praised by Hume, he has a good chance of being represented in an odious light by Dr. Lingard; and if censured by Hume, Dr. Lingard generally contrives to say a word in his recommendation.[2]

A decade later *Edinburgh Review* again made the comparison: Hume was partial to kings, Lingard to the Church.[3] Lingard was

---

1. "Antiquities of the Anglo-Saxon Church," *Quarterly Review*, VII (1812), p. 98.
2. John Allen, "Antiquities of the Anglo-Saxon Church," *Edinburgh Review,* XXV (October, 1815), p. 345.
3. Allen, "Lingard's History of England," *Edinburgh Review*, XLII, p. 4.

of course aware of Hume's preeminent place among national historians; indeed, as we have seen, to avoid his prejudices and mistakes, the historian of Hornby purposely refused to read him. Yet Lingard wrote of the review of his *History of England* in the *British Critic* that, "It does me the honour to compare my work with Hume's, . . . and owns that in some points my publication is superior."[4]

Sharon Turner was the historian closest in age and interests to Lingard. The latter, referring to Turner's uncritical treatment of St. Dunstan in his *History of the Anglo-Saxons*, wrote:

> As in other parts of his history, he excels all his prede-
> cessors in industry and accuracy; so in his account of
> St. Dunstan he has improved their incoherent fables into
> a well-connected romance.[5]

In a letter to Mawman, he was even more severe, "Between you and me, though a man of great research, he sometimes makes very silly and visionary discoveries."[6]

Two decades later Turner wrote to Lingard on the occasion of the third edition of his *Anglo-Saxon Church*, praising him highly for his method and fairness; Turner indeed admitted that he used the new edition of Lingard's work as a corrective for his own bias and errors.[7] But Lingard's tone had not softened: "Turner has sent me a present of a poem he has just published. Unfortunately that detracts from the compliment. For he is seventy-seven, and a man who publishes a poem in his seventy-seventh year must be on the high road to second childhood."[8]

Among the adverse criticisms evoked by Lingard's treatment of the reformation in his fifth volume, the longest was Robert Southey's *Book of the Church*, although as finally published it did not even mention Lingard. The latter, however, wrote it off as an apologia for the high-church Anglicans, lacking in any real re-

---

4. MS., to Robert Gradwell, February, 1821.
5. Lingard, *Anglo-Saxon Church*, (1806), II, p. 267.
6. MS., to Joseph Mawman, October, 1826.
7. April 28, 1845, quoted in Tierney, "Memoir," p. 35.
8. MS., to John Coulston, June 10, 1845.

search and largely a "compendium of Foxe" for the reformation.[9]
Yet just a few months before his death, Lingard recalled that he
had known Southey personally at Durham, and through his frequent visits to Ushaw had come to "like him very much." Indeed,
Lingard had recommended to him the *Annales Benedictinorum*.[10]

None of Lingard's contemporaries made greater use of his
History than did the man who was perhaps furthest from him in
temper and purpose, William Cobbett. Although Cobbett would
later sneer at the suggestion that he had relied on Lingard's work
for his own history of the reformation, the consensus of authority
is to the contrary.[11] Cobbett's most recent biographer, for example,
says simply that Lingard "became his primer for the History of
the Protestant Reformation."[12] In many instances, Cobbett simply
translated Lingard's neutral narrative into "his own tremendous
prose, omitted what did not suit him, and blurred out all qualifications." Although Cobbett pronounced Lingard's *History* "an ex-
cellent work, far superior to Hume," he was certain that it could
never "produce a thousandth part of the *effect* that mine will
produce in the space of three years."[13] For to Cobbett, the Catholic
historian had failed, for "like other historians, he has not informed
us of the *prices of labour* and of *food* in the several reigns." When
the British Catholic Association, in 1824, proposed to present
Cobbett with a copy of Lingard's *History*, the militant individualist
indignantly refused: "I am not to be *hallooed* on by anybody."

Henry Hallam, the first outstanding exponent of whig history,
in his *Constitutional History of England* frequently and sharply
criticized Lingard. The treatment of Anne Boleyn was overly
harsh, that of Mary Tudor too lenient.[14] Likewise, Hallam held to
be excessive Lingard's estimate, based on Tanner's *Notitia Monas-*

9. MS., to Joseph Mawman, February 14, 1824.
10. MS., to John Walker, 1851.
11. *Cobbett's Weekly Register*, LII (October 30, 1824), p. 271.
12. M. L. Pearl, *William Cobbett, a Bibliographical Account of His Life and
    Times* (London, 1953), p. 134.
13. *Cobbett's Weekly Register*, ibid.
14. Henry Hallam, *Constitutional History of England from the Accession of
    Henry VII to the Death of George II*, 5th ed. (New York, 1882), I, pp. 45,
    115.

tica, of the value of the suppressed monasteries as £142,914.[15] In summary, Hallam spoke of Lingard as an author who "cannot repress the inveterate partiality of his profession," yet one whose "acuteness and industry would otherwise have raised him to a very respectable place among our historians." The *Edinburgh Review* rather reversed the positions: "The names of Dr. Lingard and Mr. Hallam occupy a much loftier and more permanent position [than Sharon Turner]."[16] More than a decade after Hallam's *Constitutional History* appeared, Lingard read it and only then discovered the author's "great bitterness" towards him. But, he continued,

> I have taken my revenge in this manner. I have in the new edition fortified my own statement in a note here and there—and then added, "See, however, Mr. Hallam, in p.—," referring to his most offensive passages, which appear to me more disgraceful to him than to me.[17]

Dr. Lingard reserved his most biting and most disdainful comments for his most popular contemporary, Lord Macaulay, whose single reference to Lingard in the famous essay on "History" characterized him as an "apostle of Rome." The comment on Lingard in the *Edinburgh Review* by this greatest of the whig historians was amusingly revealing:

> Dr. Lingard is undoubtedly a very able and well informed writer, but whose great fundamental rule of judging seems to be, that the popular opinion on a historical question cannot possibly be correct. . . .[18]

---

15. Hallam, *ibid.*, I, p. 115 note.
16. "Antiquities of the Anglo-Saxon Church," *Edinburgh Review*, LXXXIX (April, 1849), p. 153.
17. MS., to John Coulston, July 14, 1835. In his revised treatment of Mary Tudor, Lingard appended this note: "Some writers, as Mr. Hallam, have said that the queen sought to procure an act, compelling the restoration of church property, in whatever hands it might be. The contrary is evident from the whole tenor of Pole's correspondence. Stat. iv, 274; Pole, V, 46, 51." Lingard, *History of England*, 5th ed., VII, p. 215, note.
18. Thomas B. Macaulay, "On Hallam's Constitutional History of England," *Edinburgh Review*, XLIV (October, 1826), p. 154.

The point which occasioned Macaulay's remark was Lingard's view of the Triple Alliance which Charles II signed at Breda, and Lingard, preparing his fifth edition, promised Walker, "I shall remember him when I get to that part."[19]

The day after receiving the first volumes of Macaulay's *History of England*, Lingard wrote to Coulston, "About 400 pages in Vol. I are called a History of England, but in reality contain only a string of critiques or essays. . . . There is nothing in it that calls for a word from me."[20] Lingard already had cited and criticized dispatches of the French ambassador to the court of James II which Macaulay claimed "no other writer has seen." He admitted, however, that Macaulay "has great advantage over me" in his original Dutch sources on the later Stuarts. To the suggestion that he review Macaulay's work, Lingard replied,

> For me to review him is out of the question. We are rivals as it were. It would be the "pot calling the kettle black." Occasionally I introduce passages, indirectly but not openly, designed to refute him. But I am tired of it. I find that insensibly I imitate him. I throw off the historian and become the essayist.[21]

The unusual bitterness of Lingard's view of Macaulay furnishes further reason to question the former's classification as a fellow whig historian.

Lingard's opinion of Thomas Carlyle was hardly more favorable. In 1848, referring to Carlyle's use of a spurious document concerning Cromwell's government of Ireland, Lingard wrote, "I have long looked upon Carlyle, with his Anglo-German jargon and pompous profundity, as a complete humbug."[22] He also wrote to Bishop Oliver asking for a paper in his library that might contain something on the sufferings of Ireland under Cromwell "which I might victoriously oppose to Carlyle's idolatry. . . . He

19. MS., to John Walker, May 23, 1847.
20. MS., to John Coulston, May 24(?), 1847.
21. MS., to John Walker, December 27, 1848.
22. MS., to Michael Tierney, July 24, 1848.

is a great gun among many persons and I find it necessary to
defend myself against his authority."[23] Lingard was obviously very
much aware of Carlyle's "hero historiography." When Lingard
found that Carlyle admitted Cromwell's massacres at Wexford, but
defended them on the ground that the Protector thought himself
bound in conscience to extirpate Catholicism, the historian merely
said that it was "the strangest nonsense I have ever met with."[24]

Several of the lesser historians of the period thought highly of
Lingard's work. The old priest was especially pleased, but also
amused, by the praise of one of the old "Hornby circle," Lord
Brougham:

> . . . He looks upon my history as the most surprising
> phenomenon of this age. Why so? because no one could
> possibly expect that a work so fraught with popish par-
> tiality and prejudice, could have been published in the
> 19th century. Yet, before his last departure for Cannes,
> he sent me his compliments, and to inquire after my
> health.[25]

He was likewise satisfied with the commendation of Henry Petrie,
the Keeper of the Records in the Tower, and a renowned scholar:
"The approbation of Mr. Petrie and also of Lady Spencer is highly
flattering."[26] Five years later Petrie joined Sir William Hamilton,
professor of history in the University of Edinburgh, in declaring
Lingard's *Vindication* successful as a reply to Allen. Sir Francis
Palgrave of the Record Commission, then editing the *Rolls*, several
times wrote to Lingard, both to commend his *History* and to ask
his help in establishing an exact chronology of the Parliamentary
writs.[27]

Although in the preface of his final edition, Lingard commended
Agnes Strickland, he was less polite privately: "Her writings do

---

23. MS., to George Oliver, September 1, 1848.
24. MS., to John Walker, January 29, 1848.
25. MS., to John Walker, January 5, 1845. Interestingly, Brougham never in his
    many published works mentioned Lingard.
26. MS., to Joseph Mawman, February 18, 1821.
27. MS., to Joseph Mawman, October, 1825.

not belong to that high class of literature to which history pertains. They are merely scraps from other men's productions."[28] But,

> The greatest of Miss Strickland's peccadillos is that she cares not for authority. Any anecdote which will please the readers has sufficient authority for her. She gives it as an undisputed fact. . . . In some places she has copied me word for word; people who observe the coincidence will suppose in this new edition that I have copied from her.[29]

The relative dearth of comment on Father Lingard and his writing by contemporary historians may be at least partially accounted for by their viewing him as still outside the Pale: he was a Catholic priest who for his purpose wrote history. The admission made by the *Westminster Review* in 1812, referring to Lingard's *Anglo-Saxon Church*, is indicative of a still current sentiment, "Catholic priests are not necessarily either bad citizens or bad historians."[30] To literary England of the nineteenth century, to Hallam, Macaulay, and Carlyle, to whom "Romanism" was the antithesis of all that was progressive, liberal and noble, Lingard could scarcely be considered an equal. This social and religious chasm explains the relative lack of Protestant correspondents among Dr. Lingard's writing acquaintances—and this in spite of his acceptance by the "Hornby circle" and his established moderate or impartial image.

Of the contemporary scholarly and literary periodicals, the one which most frequently and at greatest length commented on Lingard and his works was the Whig *Edinburgh Review*. We have already had occasions to note some of its many criticisms. This Whig journal manifested, through almost four decades, an increasing hostility to the Catholic historian. Yet it must be borne in mind that after the 1820's this *Review* was the special organ of Lord Macaulay, whose *History*, by 1850, was superseding Lingard's not in scholarship but certainly in popularity.

---

28. MS., to John Walker, December 5, 1849.
29. MS., to John Walker, April 27, 1849.
30. "A Vindication of Certain Passages in the Fourth and Fifth Volumes of the History of England," *Westminster Review*, VII (March, 1827), p. 188.

The first notice of Lingard in the *Edinburgh Review* occurred in 1815:

> His work [*Anglo-Saxon Church*] is the fruit of great
> labour and research. He has frequently detected, and
> exposed with success, though not without asperity, the
> errors of Protestant historians; and he has sometimes
> treated his adversaries with flippant and offensive petu-
> lance, he has on many occasions pointed out and corrected
> their misrepresentations and mistakes. We find no fault
> with his opinions, expressed with freedom and supported
> with learning, which he had advanced and defended in
> his history.[31]

But the praise is very much tempered by the quite constant
implication that any Catholic priest, even an acknowledgedly
learned one, must write sectarian history. John Allen's well-known
review of the fourth and fifth volumes of the *History of England*
included, in addition to its attack on Lingard's treatment of the
St. Bartholomew massacre, a curious blending of praise and
denunciation. While "it has deservedly placed him among the most
eminent of our English historians, . . . we can assure our clergy,
that the combat to which he provokes them, will require their
most strenuous exertions. The fabric he has raised against the
Reformation is reared by no vulgar hand."[32] Even though Lingard's
"dignity" was more noticed by the reviewer than the mechanics of
source criticism, the point was made.

The Benthamite *Westminster Review* noticed at length only
one of Lingard's works, his *Vindication*, written in defense of the
volumes on the reformation. The review began with a frank
admission:

> We acknowledge that, on the first announcement of a
> history of England from the pen of a Roman Catholic

---

31. Allen, "Antiquities of the Anglo-Saxon Church," *Edinburgh Review*, XXV,
   p. 346.
32. Allen, "Lingard's History of England," *Edinburgh Review*, XLII, p. 8.

priest, we did apprehend that neither the spirit of his religion nor the habits of his profession were calculated to prepare him for the composition of an impartial work.[33]

However, that the *Review* clearly regarded Lingard as the victor in the controversy there is no doubt: "He must take his station among the most distinguished of the writers who have investigated the annals of this country. . . . The contrast which the historian presents is truly edifying." But Lingard had small cause to boast, for the reviewer concluded that after all, "It is as difficult to be bigoted in enlightened times as it is to be liberal in bigoted times."

Examples of Tory opinion of Lingard we have already seen in the *Quarterly Review*. The general tone of this journal agreed with that of its political rivals: "This is a work of a Catholic priest, a man not unequal to his undertaking either in intelligence or research, whose . . . general perspicacity in questions of this sort we cheerfully acknowledge."[34] Significantly, the *Quarterly Review*, always very alert to an author's political affiliations, made no mention of Dr. Lingard's.

The *North British Review*, with which Lord Acton was soon associated, was generally quite favorable to Lingard; he "is a very clear and forcible writer. The work before us [Anglo-Saxon Church] displays sound judgment and great learning, and abounds in valuable information."[35] This periodical, although not professedly sectarian, had attracted to it a succession of liberal or Cisalpine Catholics, of whom Acton was the most famous and the last.

In contrast was the crude hostility of the *British Critic*: "Lingard has opened a private Still, in which he has mixed together old liquors till they appear new; and dashed and flavoured them by *surplus extractive matter*, till they have acquired an aroma fit for the gunpowder palates of his customers."[36] Equally bigoted was

---

33. "A Vindication," *Westminster Review*, VII, pp. 187-188.
34. "Lingard's History of England," *Quarterly Review*, LV (October, 1836), p. 359, note.
35. "History and Antiquities of the Anglo-Saxon Church," *North British Review*, VI (February, 1846), p. 3.
36. *British Critic*, I (February, 1827), p. 380.

the reaction of *Blackwood's Edinburgh Magazine* in an unsigned essay entitled "Dr. Lingard":

> He is a thorough Papist, and of course his work is in the thorough spirit of his blinded and unhappy faith;— venomous with the most sanctified appearance of impartiality. . . . Dr. Lingard is a man of some ability and some reading, of course a wonder in the general ignorance and dullness of the Popish writers of his time. His style is that of the cloister, monotonous, creeping, and cold.[37]

Of Lingard's presentation of the reformation, *Blackwood's* declared simply, "He treats it like a Jesuit." Further, it severely criticized the *Edinburgh Review* for "favouring" and at times praising Lingard. Surprisingly, he had "reason to be content with each. For both show that they would bite, if they *could*."[38]

The *Eclectic Review*, a sectarian organ of the dissenters, singled out the "distinguishing excellencies" of Lingard's works: their basis in original authorities and "skillful management and application of them."[39] "But the influence of his professional prejudices as a Roman Catholic clergyman is visible at every step." Alone among the contemporary journals in its adhering to a factual summary of the contents of the *History of England* was the *Monthly Review*: its sole interpretative comment was a paraphrase of Lingard's preface: "His examination of original historians has obliged him to reject many received tales."[40]

From this summary of the reaction of contemporary periodicals to Lingard and his works, it must be evident that, with the possible exception of Allen in the *Edinburgh Review*, they were little concerned with true historical criticism. The author's motives, real or imaginary, were their main interest. Also, it is interesting to note that what was surely the strongest and most original part

---

37. "Dr. Lingard," *Blackwood's Edinburgh Magazine*, XIX (March, 1826), p. 313.
38. MS., to Robert Gradwell, March 25, 1826.
39. "The History of England, by Rev. John Lingard," *Eclectic Review*, XXXIV (July, 1821), p. 23.
40. "History of England by John Lingard," *Monthly Review*, LXXXIX (July, 1819), p. 305.

of Lingard's work, his presentation of the sixteenth century, was seldom treated in reviews. These rather uniformly concentrated on criticism, such as it was, of earlier periods.

The only criticism which succeeded by its tone in surprising and irritating the historian at Hornby was Allen's review. It did so because virtually alone it questioned Lingard's veracity and acumen as an historian—in the critical use of his sources, and not, as other reviewers commonly did, simply presume his bias. After careful consultation with Joseph Mawman, his publisher, and several other confidants, Lingard decided to reply in his *Vindication*. In it he rightly noted that Allen's point of attack was a note, quite peripheral to the narrative, about the spontaneity of the St. Bartholomew Massacre in France. In a letter to George Oliver, Dr. Lingard expressed his pleasure with the more favorable tone of a later criticism in the *Edinburgh Review*: "I was told beforehand that I should be so: that it was to be so written as to make me some amends without at the same time compromising the infallibility of the reviewers."[41]

Lingard's historical writings evoked interest and criticism not only in England but also on the continent. In spite of the opposition of Bishop Milner to Lingard, and the temporary suspicion of him by Cardinal Litta of the Propaganda, the *History of England* fared well in Rome. Gradwell reported that various religious orders and houses, the pope's secretary, and several cardinals all had read it "with the highest satisfaction."[42] In spite of these favorable indications and the kindnesses of Pius VII and Leo XII, which we have already seen, Lingard was concerned over the attacks on his orthodoxy by the extreme Ultramontanist, Padre Ventura, a Theatine monk dismissed from the Sapienza by Leo XII for his unbalanced views. The *History* was purported to contain especially unsound and liberal views on papal authority, a touchy subject to Cisalpine and Ultramontanist alike.[43] Dr. Lingard was reassured, however, by a remark regarding his critics which Pope Leo was reported to have made just a few months before he died, "Why,

41. MS., to George Oliver, April 30, 1831.
42. MS., from Robert Gradwell, May 19, 1821.
43. MS., to John Bradley, January 29, 1829.

these gentlemen seem not to reflect either upon the times or the places in which the history was written."[44]

On the continent it was in France that the English historian received his widest acclaim. Already in 1826, before the *History* was completed, it was translated and published in France, but without the author's permission. He wrote to inform Mawman, "that that pirate, Galignani of Paris, has republished an edition of the *History* which he sells for £3 3s od., or 75 frs. The rascal!"[45] Yet the preface of the first French edition should have assuaged Lingard:

> The publication of Dr. John Lingard's *History of England* is one of the most remarkable events of our time; and the revolution it has produced in men's minds, not only in the country of the author, but in France and in all Europe, is such that the results promise to be lasting.[46]

In this same year, 1826, by an *Arrête Spécial* of the University of Paris, a copy of Lingard's *History of England* was ordered to be placed in every college library in France, and copies were to be given as prizes to students in philosophy and rhetoric. At this time, too, Lingard heard that Gregori, who had translated Cobbett into Italian, had done the same with the *History*.

In 1838 M. Mignet, the secretary of the French Academy proposed Lingard's election as a foreign member of the French Academy in the section of *"Histoire générale et philosophique."* Significantly, one of the other two foreign candidates proposed at this time was Leopold Ranke; the third was Gustav Geiger, professor of history at Upsala. The Archbishop of Bordeaux, sending his congratulations, assured Lingard that "it was his conviction that the 'History' had done more good to the cause of religion in France than any other work that had appeared."

By 1827 the *History* was being translated into German, and, according to Wiseman, it was the occasion of the celebrated con-

---

44. Tierney, "Memoir," p. 33.
45. MS., to Joseph Mawman, October 17, 1826.
46. John Lingard, *Abrégé de l'histoire d'Angleterre de John Lingard* (Paris, 1827), I, i.

version of Professor Phillips of the University of Berlin in 1835. The latter sent his thanks to Lingard through Wiseman, who assured Lingard, too, that the faculty of the University of Munich regarded his work very highly.[47] The even more famous German historian, Döllinger, had read Lingard's work and wanted to meet him while in England in 1837. But because of the distance to Hornby, Lingard was able to write to a friend:

> I hope Dr. Döllinger will think the conversation of his money preferable to my company. I should have been happy to have had him here in spring, as he promised to be, but I am now so very busy that I have no wish to be interrupted by him.[48]

Döllinger later wrote to Lingard that he was sorry the Englishman was not fluent in German, "and is consequently unable to profit of the historical works lately written in that language."

In the United States, too, Lingard's works were noticed. In 1841 the *Anglo-Saxon Church* was reprinted in Philadelphia; a decade later, the revised fifth edition of his *History of England* was published in Boston.[49] With the exception of *Brownson's Quarterly Review*, American periodicals generally looked very favorably upon the historian. The *Eclectic Magazine* of New York, under the title "The Late Dr. Lingard," reprinted a considerable portion of Tierney's "Memoir," and concluded:

> To Lingard's "History of England" too much praise cannot be awarded; and it has already had no ordinary share. It is, unquestionably, the very best, not only because it is the most impartial, but because it is the fullest, and the completest history.[50]

It extolled Lingard in contrast to Hume, and censured the *Edinburgh Review* for having done the opposite. The New York

---

47. MS., to F. C. Husenbeth, August 25, 1835.
48. MS., to Robert Tate, 1837.
49. MS., to Joseph Mawman, August 25, 1826; already after the second edition an American publisher suggested that an edition of the *History* be published in the United States.
50. "The Late Dr. Lingard," *Eclectic Magazine*, XXIV (November, 1851), p. 353

International Monthly Magazine termed Lingard "one of the most deservedly eminent scholars and writers of the Roman Catholic Church in England, and one of the most distinguished historians of the time."[51]

ii. A Gallican?

There emerges from a study of Lingard's relations with his fellow Catholics, and from the comments of later writers concerning that relationship, this basic question: was John Lingard a Gallican? This problem is at the center of any estimate of contemporary Catholic reaction to the historian.

The zealous American Ultramontane convert, Orestes Brownson, was very explicit in reviewing the *History of England* two years after the author's death:

> It is a learned work, it is written from the original documents, with honest intentions and rare critical sagacity; but it is not written from the Catholic point of view. The author writes as a disciple of the lowest Gallican school. . . . He writes, too, with a cold and half-skeptical spirit. He never warms, he never glows, never kindles with any enthusiasm,—he has no mellowness, and seems to grudge every concession he makes to the pious belief of his Catholic ancestors. He is the most thoroughgoing Englishman that we have ever read. . . . The reader must guard against Lingard's Gallicanism, Whiggism, and ultra-nationalism.[52]

Recent critics have been no less certain that, "It would be idle to deny that Lingard was an Old Catholic of the Old Catholics." Other estimates have been that "Lingard was English to the core," and that he "took what we may call the liberal view." Gooch states without qualification that Lingard was a Gallican.

What was Lingard's relation to the two "camps" into which English Catholics were quite distinctly divided during the first

---

51. *International Monthly Magazine*, IV (December, 1851), p. 286.
52. *Brownson's Quarterly Review*, 3rd ser., I (October, 1853), p. 544.

quarter of the nineteenth century? His position as to the respective leaders, indeed symbols, of the Cisalpines and the Ultramontanists, Charles Butler and Bishop John Milner, at least partially indicated an answer.

Lingard's acquaintance with Charles Butler began when, after Lingard's escape from France, he lived at the home of Lord Stourton, a former leader of the dissolved Catholic Committee, of which Butler was secretary. From 1793 until Butler's death in 1832, he and Lingard exchanged visits and letters, manifesting a growing friendship. At the same time, the layman was increasingly a *persona non grata* to the English ecclesiastical authorities and to the Jesuits, lately returned to Stonyhurst. Lingard's sole visit there during his first thirty years at Hornby occurred in the fall of 1812, when he defended Butler's orthodoxy to the Jesuits.

The historian was in turn often befriended by Butler, who, for example, wrote to Lingard concerning Milner's attack on the *Anglo-Saxon Church*:

> Perhaps no persons do the cause of religion more harm than those who attempt to contract the Pale of orthodoxy. . . . A wise man will not attempt it, but will be satisfied with the boundary that the faith of Christ has assigned.[53]

Butler's own estimate of Lingard's first historical work was that it was "certainly the most valuable publication written by a Catholic since Mr. Phillip's *Life of Cardinal Pole*." Later, in his *Historical Memoirs*, Butler similarly praised the *History of England*.[54] Too, the Catholic Board, the center of Cisalpine or Gallican sentiment, and whose members included Butler, Lord Holland, and the Earl of Shrewsbury, paid tribute to Lingard, while at the same time rebuffing Milner:

> Resolved unanimously
>   That the thanks of the Board of Catholics of Great Britain be given to the Rev. J. Lingard for his zealous

---

53. MS., "Charles Butler's Letter Book," British Museum, 25, 1809.
54. Charles Butler, *Historical Memoirs of the English, Irish, and Scottish Catholics since the Reformation* (London, 1822), IV, p. 456.

and successful defence of the Catholic Church in his many literary productions, and more particularly in his last able work, entitled, *A Review of Certain Anti-Catholic Publications.*

In striking contrast stood the repeated public denunciations of Lingard by Bishop John Milner. In June, 1819, for example, the bishop, in his *Orthodox Journal,* not only condemned the general spirit of Lingard's *History* by saying in summary that, "It's a bad book, Sir; only calculated to confirm Protestants in their errors," but singled out for special censure Lingard's treatment of St. Thomas a Becket. The historian's suggestion that the archbishop had become tinged with "enthusiasm" during his exile in France as well as the statement that St. Thomas was guilty of a "moment of irritation" and "precipitate measures" were pointed to by Milner as words unbecoming a Catholic. Especially, however, did he criticize Lingard's expression that the martyr died in defence of "what he thought to be his duty." "If this is not sacrificing the cause of the Church in the person of one of its canonized martyrs, I know not what is."

An anonymous pamphlet soon appeared in Lingard's defence, emphasizing that his *History* was "not a book of controversy, but a history of England."[55] Some years later the primate of Ireland, Archbishop Curtis, wrote to Lingard, telling him of Milner's efforts to persuade the Irish bishops to join him in condemning the *History*: "My answer was that we all, with our clergy and most of our educated laity, read, approved, and admired your History; ... that without that tone of impartiality adopted by you, there would be no chance of your being read."[56]

Milner was not alone among Catholics, however, in his criticisms of Lingard. A former fellow student at Douai, Richard Thompson, wrote concerning the *Anglo-Saxon Church,* "St. Augustine's 'anguish of disappointed zeal,' appears unbecoming in a saint." Another objected to Lingard's speaking of the "pious

---

55. Haile and Bonney, *Life and Letters,* p. 169. Reverend John Kirk was the most likely author.
56. MS., from Archbishop Curtis, March, 1826.

obstinacy" and "pious enthusiasm" of saints. Of the *History of England* an unsigned critic said, "It is a flowing jejune, a naked narrative of facts, already known to readers, the *protestant* part of which he appears to court . . . and from whom he has already received a meed of applause in all quarters."

Interestingly, even after Lingard's death, Catholic criticism of him was not lacking. The obituary in the *Tablet* as well as an article in the *Dublin Review* in 1855 cautioned against his liberalism. In 1866 Monsignor Talbot, criticizing Newman, wrote, "It is simply absurd in Dr. Newman to quote Lingard, Rock, and Tierney as authorities. Lingard has used expressions in his *History* which one can hardly understand how a Catholic could use them."

Lingard, on his part, was equally severe with Milner. He wrote to Walker in 1819, that the bishop "persecuted my father till his death, and since he has persecuted me. . . . He is not satisfied. He grows worse and worse. He says the book is calculated to do as much harm as good, etc. In a word, he is grown so intemperate that I have thought it prudent to have no correspondence with him.[57] Dr. Lingard was aware of Milner's efforts to get the *History* condemned by Rome, as also of the bishop's careless scholarship in his own minor tracts.[58]

Dr. Lingard's views on the issues and practices current among Catholics provide further evidence on the problem of his alleged Gallicanism. On the matter of the papal deposing power, Charles Butler wrote to Lingard in 1818:

> Talking to you confidentially I cannot help acknowledging that in the reign of Elizabeth some measures of rigour against the Catholics were excusable. The deposing Doctrine appears to me to have been universally acknowledged by all Seminary priests and religious; and their influence over the general body of Catholics was very great. . . . The grounds of distrust were naturally increased by the intrigues of Father Persons in Spain.[59]

---

57. MS., to John Orrell, May, 1807.
58. MS., to John Walker, October, 1842.
59. MS., "Charles Butler's Letter Book," March 12, 1818.

Lingard's reply revealed that he wholly agreed with Butler: the intransigence of particularly the Jesuits had forced Elizabeth's hand.[60] In the *History* he placed Campion and his fellow martyrs, Sherwin and Bryant, in a similar light:

> Their hesitation to deny the deposing power (a power then indeed maintained by the greater number of divines in Catholic Kingdoms) rendered their loyalty very problematical, in case of an attempt to enforce the bull by any foreign prince. It furnished sufficient reason to watch their behaviour with an eye of jealousy, and to require security for their good behaviour on the approach of danger, but could not justify their execution for an imaginary offense. The proper remedy would have been to offer liberty of conscience to all Catholics who would abjure the temporal pretensions of the pontiff.[61]

Lingard's treatment of Innocent III's "pretensions" with King John was equally critical.[62] To the Ultramontane, these were indeed compromisingly liberal admissions.

In 1812 the historian published a pamphlet entitled "Documents to Ascertain the Sentiments of British Catholics, in Former Ages, Respecting the Power of the Popes." His position was clear:

> . . . The opinions of former British Catholics were in unison with the oaths and declarations of their descendants at the present day: . . . "the pope of Rome neither hath nor ought to have any civil or temporal jurisdiction, power, superiority, or pre-eminence, directly or indirectly, within this realm.[63]

Nothing could have contrasted more radically with the martyred

---

60. MS., to Charles Butler, March, 1818.
61. Lingard, *History of England*, 5th ed., VIII, p. 150.
62. ". . . The servant of the servants of God became the sovereign of sovereigns, and assumed the right of judging them in his court and transferring their crowns as he thought just." Lingard, *ibid.*, III, p. 28, note.
63. John Lingard, *A Collection of Tracts on Several Subjects Connected with the Civil and Religious Principles of Catholics* (London, 1826), p. 237.

position of the Elizabethan missionary priests. To prove English refusal in medieval times of the temporal claims of the papacy, Lingard quoted three documents: a letter of William I to Gregory VII refusing homage, parliamentary rejection of Boniface VIII's claims to Scotland as a fief of the Holy See, and the renunciation by William of Gainsborough, bishop of Worcester, in 1302, of the charge of the temporalities in his diocese, although this power was given him by the papal bull of nomination.[64]

The frequent disagreements between the English vicars-apostolic and the independently-minded clergy always found Lingard among the latter. In 1837 he expressed himself as favoring the election of English bishops in chapters of the diocesan clergy. He feared, however, "It would be taken for a proof of clerical radicalism or clerical ignorance . . . at Rome."[65] Even more surprising was his favoring government surveillance of ecclesiastical correspondence with Rome.[66]

To the increasing influx into England of continental, and especially Italian, religious orders and devotions, Lingard was strongly opposed. He sarcastically suggested that a subject suitable for discussion at one of Bishop Wiseman's soirees might be "How to send away those swarms of Italian congregationalists who introduce their own customs here, and by making religion ridiculous in the eyes of protestants *prevent it from spreading here*."[67] The Jesuits, not only in the sixteenth century, but in his own day, were frequently and bitingly criticized by Lingard for their "obstinacy" and power. He was likewise opposed to their taking charge of the English College at Rome, as well as to their increase in England.[68] The pragmatism of Lingard's apologetics is difficult to gainsay:

> That there may be need of reform among us in many points I concede; but that reform should be based not on *national* customs among the Romans or Italians, but on those among Englishmen. Lights and serenading, etc. are

---

64. *Ibid.*, pp. 238-240.
65. MS., to John Walker, April 9, 1837.
66. MS., to John Kirk, March 26, 1821.
67. MS., to John Walker, February, 1850.
68. MS., to Robert Gradwell, February 20, 1824.

to foreigners in Italy the most natural manner of showing respect; not so with us. Our great object should be to extend the catholic religion among us, and for that purpose I hold it necessary to make converts among the higher of the middle classes of society. . . . If this be the case, we are bound in conscience to eliminate everything unnecessary that is calculated to indispose such persons from joining us, or to augment their antipathy to us.[69]

During the last decade of his life, Dr. Lingard realized his increasing isolation in the changing character and spirit of English Catholicism: Wiseman, the Jesuits, the Oxfordians—all convinced him that "the best thing that I can do is to keep myself to myself."[70]

To the English historian, the Irish Catholics were overly emotional and rebellious. He criticized the Irish bishops for "constantly reminding the masses that, if they are miserable, it is owing to the English."[71] In the 1820's he had disapproved of O'Connell's direct, public methods in accomplishing Catholic emancipation; Lingard preferred the more gradual personal, indirect approach. In this light he viewed his friendship with Brougham, for example.

A final source of evidence regarding Lingard's Gallicanism lies in his relations to the "Second Spring": to Wiseman and the Oxford Movement. The future cardinal, when he was still editor of the *Dublin Review*, reiterated Milner's objection to Lingard's attributing "religious enthusiasm" to Thomas of Canterbury. The restoration of the hierarchy in 1850 also was a source of disagreement between Wiseman and Lingard, who especially criticized what appeared to him as a lack of prudence and moderation in the new cardinal's famous "Pastoral from outside the Flaminian Gate." Likewise Lingard looked with disfavor on Wiseman's encouragement of religious orders and "foreign" practices and devotions, as we have seen. Yet these disagreements were but indications of a deeper divergence between Lingard, representing the liberal, independent, isolated days of the penal laws, and the new, confident

---

69. MS., to John Walker, February, 1850.
70. MS., to John Walker, 1842.
71. MS., to John Walker, January 27, 1848.

Oxfordians—the Wisemans, Newmans, Mannings. Lingard's season was the pre-emancipation age; Wiseman's was the Second Spring. The Catholic of the earlier era never forgot that he was equally an Englishman, content with what he considered the "essentials" of his religion, and impatient with the "non-essentials" of foreign pietism.

These disagreements, both in detail and in spirit, with the aging historian, however, did not prevent Wiseman from holding him in high regard. Just a few months before Lingard's death, the cardinal wrote to him:

> Be assured of my affectionate gratitude to you . . . for the great, important, and noble services which you have rendered to religion through life, and which have so much contributed to overthrow error, and give a solid historical basis to all subsequent controversy with Protestantism.[72]

To the Oxford converts, those phenomena of the closing decade of his life, Lingard had no link. By 1848, their "wordiness and dreaminess," their "enthusiasms," repelled this product of the Age of Reason.[73] To Walker he admitted, "I have not read Newman, nor Oakley, nor could ever get through any one of Ward's productions. They are all inconceivably lengthy and tiresome." Especially was Lingard wary of the "foreign forms of devotion" and the liturgical emphasis which he associated with the Tractarians; he judged their aim was to "transform Englishmen into Romans."

Although it is probably true that Lingard was too wary of the Oxford Movement, it was only because he represented the Catholicism of the catacombs and could never shake off entirely the mentality of the penal laws. Fundamental, too, was Lingard's conviction, born of his historical study, that the Catholicism of Wiseman and Newman was not a rebirth, a "Second Spring," but merely the continuation of the same, unbroken English Catholic

---

72. Tierney, "Memoir," in Lingard, *History of England*, 6th ed., I, p. 31.
73. MS., to John Walker, April 27, 1848.

tradition implanted by St. Augustine of Canterbury fifteen centuries before.[74]

From an examination of Lingard's relations to Butler and Milner and the attitudes they personified, from Lingard's views of current Catholic issues and practices, and finally from his relation to the Second Spring, an answer to the question of his Gallicanism may be offered. Indeed, in the light of the justified distinction between full-blown Gallicanism and its moderated English counterpart, Cisalpinism, the solution comes quite spontaneously. John Lingard, both in the estimate of his contemporaries, and in the longer perspective, was a Cisalpine. On no important point and in no measurable degree did his views on the crucial issues differ from those of Charles Butler. And conversely, virtually every matter, including the presentation of historical research, found Lingard and John Milner diametrically opposed. However, Lingard's "Gallicanism" also partially resulted from his consciously apologetic approach and presentation; his "concessions" were often more on the level of psychology than of doctrine. Yet as Cisalpinism waned after 1829, the historian at Hornby was increasingly isolated and out of touch with the Catholics of his later years. Surely to the zealous Ultramontanist Brownson, Lingard was a Gallican.

To estimate John Lingard's direct influence on his contemporaries is difficult, his indirect influence impossible. Gradwell reported from Rome that there the *History of England* was spoken of as a major cause of the improving status of Catholics in that country. Twenty-five years later, a letter from Darcy Talbot in London allowed Lingard to write to Walker that,

> Talbot adds that it is the opinion of many there, that my history had no small share in creating in the universities the spirit of enquiry into Catholic matters, which had led by degrees to the conversion of so many collegians. This, if it be true, is very gratifying.[75]

---

74. This was the general theme of, e.g., John Lingard, *Strictures on Dr. Marsh's "Comparative View of the Churches of England and Rome"* (London, 1815), pp. 1-88.
75. MS., to John Walker, 1849.

Indeed, shortly after Lingard's death, a protestant reviewing Froude's *History of England* reluctantly admitted that, "Lingard is now actually recommended as a standard authority for the young, by educated Protestants."[76] Nothing could have better fulfilled Lingard's motive or justified his approach; nothing better substantiates Gooch's judgment that Lingard's *History* "remained the most popular sketch of our history till the appearance of Green."

Only a public that still read the classics, Hazlitt, Lamb, Brougham, and Gibbon could at least in part appreciate an historian distinguished by research and moderation. Hence, "he was able to occupy a position in general English life such as no Catholic priest had occupied for centuries." Yet fundamentally John Lingard was out of step with his contemporaries: as an historian critically using original sources, he strode ahead; as a Catholic at times excessively influenced by his earlier years and the liberal atmosphere, he lagged behind.

---

76. "Froude's History of England," *North British Review*, LI (November, 1856), p. 74.

CHAPTER VI

THE ENGLISH RANKE

The historiographical and religious world, the motives, and particularly the method, of John Lingard are now familiar. But none of these are historiographically satisfying in the abstract. How did their practical effects combine in Lingard's writing? How did Dr. Lingard treat an entire historical period or subject? How did he, in view of his motives, and using his distinctive method, approach a major era or movement in the concrete?

And finally: the English Ranke. The great German "founder" of scientific history also wrote of the English reformation some four decades after Lingard's first edition. What are the points of comparision? Ranke, in spite of "the rise, decline, and persistence" of his reputation, remains on a high historiographical pedestal; is John Lingard rightly ranked with him?

These, then, are the questions that remain: (i) how did Lingard distinctively treat a specific, concrete historical period? and (ii) how truly is he the English Ranke?

i. Lingard and the Sixteenth Century

John Lingard devoted three volumes of the last edition of his *History of England* to the sixteenth century. These, by general consensus, contain, in Peardon's words, the historian's "most original work." Likewise, it was certainly Lingard's treatment of the reformation, the distinguishing phenomenon of the sixteenth century, that elicited the most violent and continuing comment on the *History*. Further, this portion of Lingard's work has best stood the proverbial test of time: Conyers Read, G. R. Elton, Philip Hughes, J. E. Neale, E. Harris Harbison lead the twentieth century historians of the English reformation who continue to cite and commend Lingard.[1] Thus, if any one entire era or period is to be selected as illustrative of Lingard's approach, the century of the Tudors seems the natural, indeed necessary, choice.

What perhaps most distinguishes Lingard's presentation of this controversial century is its very lack of distinction. He offended Milner and militant Catholics by neutrality and omission; he irritated John Allen and other Protestant controversialists by quiet, undramatic factual statements. Neither camp could accuse Lingard of a "philosophical" or overtly interpretative view of the reformation. To Lingard's treatment of this crucial and controversial century Allen's criticism clearly applied: "Revolutions the most important glide before us, without any anticipation of their approach, notice of their arrival, or retrospective view of their effects."

Lingard does not propose in his *History* a general view or interpretative synthesis of the English reformation. Rather, Henry VIII's difficulties and final break with the Church emerge from Lingard's pages of quite purely political history unannounced and unintroduced. Indeed, Lingard presents not a synthesis or interpretation but an unembellished narrative, largely chronological and political, of the sixteenth century. He succeeded with amazing consistency in adhering to his promise: "I shall narrate the facts with impartiality; the reader must draw his own conclusions." Philip Hughes, in the 1950's, still in scholarly awe of Lingard, suggested, "Lest his own language accidentally colour the facts he is relating, and so turn his history into apologetic, Lingard will deliberately choose a cold, detached style."[2] Perhaps the closest that Lingard came to permitting himself an interpretive evaluation

---

1. E.g., Philip Hughes in his now standard *Reformation in England* (New York, 1950-1954), II, p. 265, quoting Lingard's cautious conclusion, "With whom the persecution under Mary originated is a matter of uncertainty," remarks, "Lingard's words are still true. Another 130 years of scholarship have not added substantially to what he wrote in 1823."

2. Hughes, *ibid.*, III, p. 241. Almost amusing is the very recent comment on Hughes' own style: "At times Hughes' work attains the level of history of the absurd . . . with its penchant for minute detail . . . which is certainly not unintentional, but instead represents a most subtle kind of Catholic apologetic." Norman F. Cantor, *The English* (New York, 1967), p. 380. This precise criticism had been leveled at Lingard.

in the era occurred in the paragraphs about Elizabeth and her Parliaments: The Queen's

> obstinacy was productive of one advantage to the nation; it put an end to that tame submission to the will of the sovereign, which had characterized and disgraced the parliaments under the dynasty of the Tudors. The discontent of the nation burst forth in defiance of every restraint imposed by the government. . . .[3]

Even a most careful reading of Lingard's pages on sixteenth century England—her break with Rome, the new "strong" monarchy, the religious vacillations—will not reveal even guarded generalizations or tentative hypotheses. Of the English reformation's broader causes and consequences, of its deeper nature, there is no explicit word. Of course, this mode of presentation was, as we have seen, not accidental, but quite intended. What remains impressive is that the author was so consistent in his restraint and reticence.

Although Lingard, in one of his lesser writings, referred to the reformation as a "break" in English tradition, no overt development of his view appeared in his *History*. In the obvious sense that the split from Rome was a departure from traditional faith and religious affiliation, the sixteenth century upheaval constituted for him a "break in tradition." And even this the reader must see for himself. However, in two corollaries Dr. Lingard had found later scholarly company. His view that the Act of Supremacy of 1533 severed a five-century long tradition of canonical appeals and dependence on Rome found later famous substantiation in Maitland. Praemunire, by having to forbid the practice, testified to its existence. Lingard's unobtrusive suggestion that Thomas Cromwell's project would vest in the crown supreme jurisdiction has found convincing support in G. R. Elton, whose famous "Tudor revolution" begins not in 1485, but in 1536, and, even more recently, in A. G. Dickens.[4] Ranke, in his later English history, attributed no

---

3. Lingard, *History of England*, 5th ed., VII, p. 355.
4. G. R. Elton, *The Tudor Revolution in Government* (Cambridge, 1953), and A. G. Dickens, *The English Reformation* (New York, 1964).

unique plan or awareness to Cromwell; in fact, he quite ignored him.

Lingard's leading predecessor and contemporaries were not so reticent in advancing philosophical or interpretative views of the reformation. David Hume, the most popular national historian until Lingard, introduced the reformation by stating bluntly, "Few ecclesiastical establishments have been fixed upon a worse foundation than that of the church of Rome, or have been more hurtful to the peace and happiness of mankind." The controlling religious convictions of Lingard's contemporary, Sharon Turner, were repeatedly no less strident. Even Henry Hallam, in his *Constitutional History*, showed little restraint in advancing his view of the general nature of the religious revolt. He looked upon the split with Rome not as a break in tradition but as a return to scriptural religion and to individual emancipation "from the thraldom of ecclesiastical jurisdiction."

It was, however, in the greatest of the whig historians, Lord Macaulay, that opinionated synthesis reached its eloquent peak. Its very style justifies full quotation:

> Those who hold that the influence of the Church of Rome in the dark ages was, on the whole, beneficial to mankind, may yet with perfect consistency regard the Reformation as an inestimable blessing. The leading strings, which preserve and uphold the infant, would impede the full-grown man. . . . The child who teachably and undoubtingly listens to the instructions of his elders is likely to improve rapidly. But the man who should receive with childlike docility every assertion and dogma uttered by another man no wiser than himself would become contemptible. . . . Hence, that dominion which, during the dark ages, had been, in spite of many abuses, a legitimate and salutary guardianship, became an unjust and noxious tyranny.[5]

Froude, writing a half-century after Lingard's first edition, merely echoed Macaulay's condemnations.

---

5. Thomas B. Macaulay, *History of England*, I, pp. 36-37.

Hence, the very lack of subjective or partisan interpretation made Lingard's treatment of the reformation "original." To omit what Hume called "a short digression" (of some hundred pages) on the general nature of the revolt was itself an historical novelty. Lingard declined his publisher's suggestion that he include "a dissertation on the consequences of the reformation: I do not see that it is necessarily connected with my subject."[6] Apart from mere chroniclers, it may be impossible to write history with fewer personal intrusions and flourishes than Lingard's narrative of reformation England.

In the matter of organization or periodization of both the entire scope of English history and of the sixteenth century, Lingard's *History* revealed few innovations. His principle of periodization was basically chronological; reigns, not movements or trends or doctrines, determined volumes and chapters. This, of course, posed less a problem in sixteenth century England, where each reign virtually coincided with a change of doctrine or political posture. Of the works contemporary with Lingard's, only Hallam's *Constitutional History* and Macaulay's *History of England from the Accession of James II* differed markedly in organization, and these for obvious reasons.

More detailed insight into Lingard's presentation of the sixteenth century may be gained also from a comparison of his evaluation, with those of contemporary historians, of some of the outstanding, controversial personages of the era. It was, after all, in many ways, a "time of giants."

Certainly no character of the reformation was more an enigma than Thomas Cranmer, and none was more crucial. Lingard's position on several celebrated, controverted incidents was clear. Whereas both Hume and Turner wholly omit the embarrassing subject of Cranmer's famous consecration oath, Lingard asked bluntly,

> But by what casuistry could the archbishop elect, who was well acquainted with the services expected from him, reconcile it with his conscience to swear at his consecra-

---

6. MS., to Joseph Mawman, December 1, 1820.

tion canonical obedience to the pope, when he was already resolved to act in opposition to the papal authority?[7]

In answer, Lingard permitted himself only this personal comment, "I will only observe that oaths cease to offer any security if their meaning may be qualified by previous protestations, made without the knowledge of the party who is principally interested."[8] His array of authorities and evidence, which included Strype's *Memorials*, Wilkins' *Concilia*, the *State Papers*, and the *Statutes of the Realm*, permitted but one conclusion: Archbishop Cranmer was clearly guilty of open and deliberate duplicity. Hallam, though he took cognizance of the incident, did not presume to interpret it.

The archbishop's character emerged from Lingard's pages with little to commend it. Duplicity in his oath, immorality in his clandestine marriage, opportunism in his politics, and vacillation in his religious doctrine marred the man. Lingard's leading contemporary, Sharon Turner, was evidently aware of the almost impossible difficulties of narrating, let alone praising, Cranmer's career. Hence, incredible though it be, Turner, in his four volumes on the reformation, never once so much as mentioned or referred to Cranmer! This is surely evidence by silence.

For a Catholic historian who attempts to be impartial, Thomas Cranmer is the test. Even the account of the archbishop's preparation of the *Second Book of Common Prayer* remained neutral and almost too brief in its coolness:

> Taking the Latin missals and breviaries, they omitted such parts as they deemed superfluous or superstitious, translated others, and by numerous additions and corrections endeavored to meet the wishes of the new teachers, without shocking the belief or the prejudices of their opponents.[9]

Privately, in contrast, Dr. Lingard admitted that, "I think I can

---

7. Lingard, *History of England*, 5th ed., VI, p. 191.
8. *Ibid.*, p. 193.
9. *Ibid.*, VII, p. 29.

show that Cranmer had prepared . . . to burn the believers in Transubstantiation. He got no more than he meant to inflict."[10]

With Lingard's contemporaries certainly the most universally unpopular person associated with the English reformation was "Bloody" Mary Tudor. The estimate of Turner may be taken as typical: "Her name stands on the rolls of English history like the pharos on the dark and dangerous rock, to warn every potentate and country, what must be timelily [sic] discerned and shunned." And although Hume, Turner, Hallam, and Lingard all agreed in citing Lord Burghley's statistics concerning the Marian persecutions, as found in Strype's *Memorials*, they differed markedly in their interpretations. Dr. Lingard pointed out, citing also the testimony of Stowe and Noialles, that Mary was actually extremely lenient in her policy towards heretics when she first came to the throne—"an instance of clemency, considering all the circumstances, not perhaps to be paralleled in the history of those ages." However—and here he was truly an innovator as a Catholic— Lingard severely criticized the "intolerance" of Catholic Mary, but he placed it in its times:

> The foulest blot on the character of this queen is her long and cruel persecution of the reformers. . . . It is but fair, however, to recollect that the extirpation of erroneous doctrine was inculcated as a duty by the leaders of every religious party. Mary only practiced what they taught. It was her misfortune, rather than her fault, that she was not more enlightened than the wisest of her contemporaries.[11]

He demonstrated that Mary chose as her husband Philip of Spain at the urging of the Emperor Charles and against the advice of Bishop Gardiner.[12] Still, to the fires of Smithfield, to the admittedly forbidding personality of the queen, Lingard's narrative remained cool and crowded.

As Mary was criticized, Elizabeth was praised by Lingard's

---

10. MS., to John Kirk, January, 1821.
11. Lingard, *History of England*, 5th ed., VII, p. 242.
12. MS., to William Poynter, October 29, 1822.

contemporaries, and indeed by our own as well. The ludicrous extremes to which one historian's adulations went appeared in Turner:

> "Hospitality, charity and splendour" were the characteristics of her household, and upon the most liberal and comprehensive plan; embracing the inferior as well as the superior orders of society. . . . She gratified her subjects by calling frequent parliaments; and had the pleasure of always witnessing their affectionate loyalty. . . . She had so little of personal pride, and such a desire to promote the public good, that "she would not refuse the informations of mean persons, if they were given with purposes of improvement. . . . Her piety appeared in all her transactions and conduct. She was seldom absent from the public prayers and divine services. She passed much time in reading the Scriptures, and the Fathers; she often composed prayers when the occasion required."[13]

To Hume, Elizabeth "enjoyed a natural frugality of temper, . . . singular felicity . . . and a judicious and vigorous perseverance." James Anthony Froude proclaimed eloquently but ambiguously, "She was the idol of the young, the restless, the enthusiastic; her name had been identified with freedom; and she detested more sincerely than any theologian living, the perversity which treated opinion as a crime."

Lingard's portrait, by contrast, was cold and unenthusiastic. He portrayed her, quoting the *State Papers*, Camden, Stowe, Strype, and D'Ewes, as essentially a pragmatist, a diplomat in religious matters. He noted critically both "the historians who celebrate the golden days of Elizabeth" as well as "the dismal picture of national misery, drawn by the Catholic writers of the same period. Both have taken too contracted a view of the subject."[14] Lingard's estimate of Elizabeth, and particularly of her religious beliefs and policy, has found wide and general support in more recent writers. Read and Knappen, for example, agree substantially with Neale,

---

13. Sharon Turner, *History of England* (London, 1838), XII, pp. 598-599.
14. Lingard, *History of England*, 5th ed., VIII, p. 429.

who speaks of the "Queen's mind, with its secular view of the problem . . . was essentially modern." Lingard, however, was sympathetic to Elizabeth's opposition to the papal disposing power and to the Jesuits who espoused it.

Concerning one salient character of the sixteenth century there existed between Lingard and his fellow historians surprising unanimity. To Hume, Hallam, Turner, Macaulay, and Lingard alike, Cardinal Wolsey was distinguished by unrivaled, unchecked ambition and vain-glory. Turner's characterization was, as usual, distinguished for its unrestraint, when he contrasted Wolsey to Caesar Borgia, to the latter's advantage.

Lingard said simply that the cardinal's "love of wealth was subordinate only to his love of power."[15] Yet Lingard conceded that,

> The best eulogy on his character is to be found in the
> contrast between the conduct of Henry before, and after
> the cardinal's fall. As long as Wolsey continued in favour,
> the royal passions were confined within certain bounds.

Recent scholarship has revised these older views of Wolsey surprisingly little. His chief biographer, Albert Pollard, after surveying the historiography of the cardinal, portrays him as a statesman, not a theologian, as given to almost pitiable pride, but "indefatigable."

Possibly no action by the Henrician government evoked stronger emotions than the dissolution of the monasteries. Their wholesale suppression, economically and politically most understandable, was an essential part in Cromwell's plan to vest supreme authority in the crown. Even David Hume, strongly anti-clerical though he was, made no issue about Henry's motives: "As it was known that the King's intention in this visitation was to find a pretence for abolishing monasteries, we may naturally conclude, that the reports of the commissioners are very little to be relied on."[16] Dr. Lingard, indeed, was personally far more critical of the

---

15. *Ibid.*, VI, p. 41.
16. David Hume, *The History of England from the Invasion of Julius Caesar to the Revolution in 1688* (New York, n.d.), II, p. 123.

monasteries and correspondingly willing to accept some of the damaging charges against them: "the monks of that period were men of little reputation and had entirely degenerated from the spirit of their original institutes . . . a degenerate, time-serving class of men."[17]

Having gone so far privately, Lingard impartially described the directives and men commissioned by Cromwell to investigate the religious houses. The example of Germany had proved that the Church could be "plundered with impunity," and Cromwell had "long ago" promised this as a result of supremacy. Cromwell's suggestion was welcomed by Henry, "whose thirst for money was not exceeded by his love of power." No less, the Lords of the Council, hungry for land amid the enclosures, expected a share. Finally, Archbishop Cranmer feared the monasteries as the firmest center of the old, international faith.[18]

Lingard reserved one of his rare sarcasms for the question of why the smaller and poorer monastic houses were investigated and suppressed before the greater: "To some men it appeared contrary to experience, that virtue should flourish most where the temptations to vice were more numerous, and the means of indulgnce more plentiful."[19] Then he explained: the abbots and priors of the wealthy foundations were in the Lords to protect themselves for the moment. Lingard's estimate of the value of the confiscated monastic lands as £142,914, based on Tanner's *Notitia Monastica*, called excessive by Hallam, was far under the actual worth. By 1547, "some two-thirds of the vast plunder had already been alienated. . . . The crown received in moneys £779,700."[20]

The unique value of Lingard's narrative of the century of the reformation rests on its sources. In the discovery and critical use of manuscript and printed, domestic and foreign primary documents, Lingard's work on the sixteenth century was novel in his day and remained so for at least two generations. The rich variety of sources quoted for Mary's reign, for example, included the con-

17. MS., to John Kirk, November 25, 1820.
18. Lingard, *History of England*, 5th ed., VI, pp. 230-231.
19. *Ibid.*, p. 232.
20. Hughes, *Reformation in England*, I, p. 328.

temporary chronicles of Stowe, Holinshed, Burnet, Foxe, and Strype; Somer's Tracts: Howell's *State Trials*; Cardinal Pole's manuscript letters; the dispatches of the French ambassador to England, Noailles, and of the Imperial ambassador, Renard; as well as the two contemporary Italian works of Rosso and Pollini.[21]

Dr. Lingard was the first modern historian to use the Harleian *Miscellany* and the Lansdowne manuscripts in the British Museum.[22] J. E. Neale recognizes him as first to employ the Southwell papers, existing in manuscript at Stonyhurst; likewise, he utilized the Burleigh and Hardwick *State Papers*.[23] Here he stands immeasurably above his contemporaries Turner, Hallam, and Macaulay; in fact, only James Anthony Froude, almost fifty years later, rivals him—and his scholarship was marred by his chronic and proverbial inaccuracy. Surely Ranke's exploitation of the Venetian archives find their full counterpart in Lingard's innovating and critical use of this wealth of sixteenth century documents.

The significance of Lingard's treatment of the sixteenth century consisted, then, both in his refusal to philosophize and interpret generally the period, and in his cautious views, based on a wealth of original sources, of the critical persons of the age. His approach, though often lacking drama and "originality" in presentation, has been sustained and justified to a remarkable degree. His narration of this century, in contrast to those of Hume, Turner, and Hallam, retains more than a historiographical importance.

ii. The English Ranke?

In 1885 George Bancroft told the American Historical Association what it already knew: that Leopold von Ranke was "the greatest living historian." From that time to our own, from Acton and Feuter to von Laue and Geyl, Ranke has remained, despite his critics, the personification of scientific history. His place, in Lord Acton's words, as "the real originator of the heroic study of records" is proverbial. This by no means to ignore either what

---

21. Lingard, *History of England*, 5th ed., VII, pp. 110-138.
22. MSS., to Joseph Mawman, June 4, 1820, and September 1, 1822.
23. MS., to John Kirk, December 20, 1820.

Ferdinand Schevill called the "rise, decline, and persistence" of Ranke's reputation or the possible validity of his critics' arguments.

Here, however, Leopold von Ranke is the norm: this is not the place to exegete or defend him. Both he and his ideas are too well known and long discussed to need explanation or proof. Our purpose is not to question or quibble concerning his status or greatness; if one disagrees with the standard, that is not our concern here. But that Ranke has been held for a century as the standard of success in historical method, right or wrong, is beyond cavil. Even less can it be our aim to imply John Lingard's superiority: that would surely be begging the question.

Rather, the object here is much more modest—to suggest a few points of comparison, to seek out areas of possible similarity between the rightly famous Ranke and the far lesser known Lingard, keeping in mind that the English historian in his productive years antedated the German by a decade or so.

When inquiry into the motives of the objective Ranke seems almost redundant, the results are all the more surprising. Just prior to publishing his first volumes of his *History of the Popes*, he wrote that his desire to study the past had been stimulated by a religious preoccupation: "It was this and this alone which drove me to historical research."[24] From Venice in 1829, amid his initial work in the archives he made famous, he confided to his brother, "I know that I am on that road which God has prescribed for me. I am in that position which I need. How good is He, our Creator. . . . Here I am, among the least, and experience the signs of his charitable hand on myself."[25] "Through the sheer exhausting mass of documents, behind the record of man's history, Ranke saw the hand of God. That was the inexhaustible source of his persistence."[26] Although he approached the history of the popes as a subject which was in itself "a thought of God,"[27] he did so strictly to find historical truth: "Popery can now inspire us with no other

---

24. Herbert Butterfield, *Man on His Past* (Cambridge, 1955), p. 138.
25. Theodore Von Laue, *Leopold Ranke: the Formative Years* (Princeton, 1950), p. 41.
26. *Ibid.*, p. 42.
27. Leopold von Ranke, *History of the Popes* (London, 1927), III, p. 174.

interest than what results from the development of its history and its former influence."[28]

We find, then, even in Leopold von Ranke a motive beyond simply recreating the past. That he searched history to find God by no means perverted or prostituted his research or the products of it.

Ranke was almost Augustinian in his overt recognition of Providence in history; he spoke of it far more frequently and casually than the technical historian of today. He concluded the famous preface to his first work, the *History of the Latin and Germanic Nations*: "The main thing is always what we deal with . . . humanity as it is, comprehensible or inexplicable, the life of the individual, of generations, of nations, and at times the hand of God above them."[29] Even in the narrative he did not hesitate to assign historical causality to God. He described the military force of the Emperor Maximilian as so mighty that "neither Europe nor Asia could have resisted him. But God gave that it was used for freedom rather than for domination."[30] Even the discovery of America was "a gift of God."

The historian must aim at "the intuitive understanding of the cosmos; never was the past "the work of blind destiny." Such statements are, of course, non-existent, indeed inconceivable, in Lingard. True history to Ranke "was a mixture of the best of Niebuhr, who in all his art of individual research lacked universality, with the best of Hegel, who with his profound universality lacked the thorough grasp of the individual fact."[31] By these standards, Lingard's model would have been Neibuhr alone.

Leopold von Ranke fittingly culminated his life work with the nine volumes of *World History*. Even his earlier writings, dealing as they did with a succession of individual nations at the opening of modern times, were conceived in their broader setting. Although he was accused of being overly Prussian, and that his view of the world was limited severely to western Europe, universal or "gen-

---

28. *Ibid.*, I, p. xxii.
29. Von Laue, *Ranke*, p. 29.
30. *Ibid.*
31. *Ibid.*, p. 123.

eral" history, as he called it, was his framework. Just as the earlier Göttingen school, Ranke wanted to rescue universal history from the philosophers.

For a scholar whose hallmark was objectivity and detachment, Ranke was often immersed in German politics. After the 1830 revolts he was chosen to be the spokesman for Prussia and particularly her German policy; he accepted the editorship of a new, semi-official periodical designed to explain or propagate it. Although he was not Prussian by birth, he was conditioned by his years at Berlin. The twin floods of post-Napoleonic nationalism and liberalism surrounded and touched him. But not only was he a political publicist for a time, but even more a widely read student of political philosophy: Herder, Schlegel, Goethe, Hegel. Ranke's famous *Dialogue on Politics* demonstrated both his theoretical interests and practical involvements. His political affiliations were not difficult to discern. And this in the man with whom historical detachment is equated—surely a far cry from the vicar of Hornby whose preference for the Whigs must be guessed from the politics of his friends and a few brief private letters.

It is, certainly, in the "cult of the document" that Ranke's reputation stands highest and most distinctively. The preface to his 1824 *History of the Latin and Germanic Nations* contained his dictum: history "wants only to show what actually happened" (*wie es eigentlich gewesen*). And further, "The strict presentation of facts, contingent and unattractive though they may be, is undoubtedly the supreme law. After this, it seems to me, comes the exposition of the unity and progress of events."[32] The text of this first of Ranke's histories was based on "memoirs, diaries, letters, diplomatic reports, and original narratives of eyewitnesses." Just as Lingard, Ranke cautioned without changing, "Will it not often seem harsh, disconnected, colorless, and tiring?" And as Lingard, he declined to introduce his narrower subject with "a general description of the political institutions of Europe."

While the preface to his first work contained Ranke's most quoted principle, the appendix to the same book was an essay "On

---

32. Fritz Stern, ed., *The Varieties of History* (New York, 1956), p. 57.

the Criticism of Writers of Modern History" which to many inaugurated modern critical historiography. However, the narrative of the *History* Ranke based not on manuscript but printed sources. Only from about 1840 did he conclude that the sixteenth century could not be written from printed records only. By that time, Lingard's volumes on the reformation were almost two decades old.

The Germany in which Leopold Ranke was educated was the center of classical philology. Niebuhr was one of its famous masters, Ranke a most enthusiastic and apt student. It was, in fact, the methods of philology that he applied to modern history. Eighteenth century philology influenced Ranke no more, however, than the spirit of the succeeding romantic idealism: by both particularly his earlier works were noticeably marked. He utilized a meticulous method "to touch the divine."

That much of Ranke's immediate and enduring reputation as the founder of scientific history was due to the sixty-three volumes which he authored is obvious; but a very considerable portion of his fame rested in his seminar at the University of Berlin and the "pupils" he trained there. Not only giants as Waitz and Sybel, but more than three generations of historians studied under him. His followers filled the academic chairs throughout Germany and in England and America as well. He did not live beyond the Pale, nor were his motives suspect.

By the mid-1850's Professor Ranke was working on the last of his national histories, *A History of England Principally in the Seventeenth Century.* Of the six volumes, he devoted the first largely to the century of the reformation. Previously, he had introduced his *History of the Reformation in Germany* by reflecting philosophically:

The ideas by which human conditions are founded contain the divine and eternal element from which they spring, yet never completely. For a time they are benevolent, life-giving; new creations pass from under their breath. However, nothing on earth reaches perfection. Nothing, therefore, is immortal. When the time has been fulfilled, tendencies of great spiritual consequence arise from the decay, which destroy it completely. Such is the fate of God's creations in the world.[33]

Now, he viewed England's part "in the work of emancipating the world from the rule of the western hierarchy."[34] Just as Lingard, however, his "main interest lies in the political transformation" in England—in contrast to the conflict of doctrines in reformation Germany. "In England, the monarchy perfectly understood its position in relation to this great change."[35]

Protestant critics of his earlier *History of the Popes* had regretted his dispassionate treatment of Protestantism's foes. About his characterization of Mary Tudor they had little to complain: the queen "had no sympathy for the life, the interests, the struggles of her people: she hated them from her childhood. . . . No excuse can free her memory from the dark shade which rests on it."[36] The Catholic Bishop Bonner of London was "fanatical. . . , almost bloodthirsty," whereas her victims "showed a sublime contempt of death." His analysis of the motives that prompted the confiscation of the monasteries was incisive but more impartial: "In the rules they followed, in the Orders to which they belonged, the intercommunication of Latin Christianity had its most living expression; but it was exactly this which the King and Parliament wished to sever."[37] Their dissolution was a "necessary sacrifice to the unity of the country and at the same time the greed of great men." To Thomas Cromwell he attributed no special place in the monastic story.

In his volume on the sixteenth century, Ranke cited Hallam and Froude, and surprisingly, Sharon Turner, as well as Strype, Foxe, and Labanoff among the primary sources. There is mention neither of Lingard nor of sources which he was first to use, the Harleian *Miscellany* or the Lansdowne manuscripts.

---

33. Leopold von Ranke, *History of the Reformation in Germany* (New York, 1905), I, p. 40.
34. Leopold von Ranke, *A History of England Principally in the Seventeenth Century* (New York, 1966), I, p. vi.
35. *Ibid.*
36. *Ibid.*, p. 209.
37. *Ibid.*, p. 158.

Ironically, the past "as it actually happened"—with its traditional though perhaps mistaken implications of uninterpreted factualness—can be more commonly found in Lingard than in Ranke. The latter was much more inclined to paint the bigger canvas, to interpret and philosophize. Ranke was essentially the universal historian who saw the struggles of the sixteenth century in terms of "ideas" or principles; Lingard saw them as fundamentally a conflict of persons and events.

Ranke's reputation was made and still rests primarily on his method, particularly his search for documents and his critical use of them. This is the common ground—heurisic and criticism—that he and Lingard share. In this sense, in this area, John Lingard was the English Ranke. In historical synthesis or presentation the analogy weakens: here the German consciously drew in bolder strokes segments of what he saw as "general history"; Lingard's history remained essentially national and narrative.

On so many scores—motive, philosophy, universal history, political involvement, influence—Lingard had little in common with Ranke. But by the one criterion that made each initially accepted and remains their hallmark—method—they bear comparison. What Lord Acton said of Ranke may without substantial change be applied to Lingard: "He has obtained so much new matter at Paris, Oxford, in the British Museum, and the Record Office, that he is entirely free from conventional influences."[38]

---

38. *Home and Foreign Review*, VI (April, 1864), p. 715.

NOTE ON PRIMARY AUTHORITIES

The two major works of John Lingard provided the most necessary and valuable source for this study. *The Antiquities of the Anglo-Saxon Church* (Newcastle, 1806), 2 vols., was thoroughly recast and revised in *The History and Antiquities of the Anglo-Saxon Church*, 2nd ed. (London, 1845), 2 vols. *The History of England from the First Invasion by the Romans to the Accession of William and Mary* (London, 1819-1830), 8 vols., was four times subsequently revised by the author, in 1823-1831, 1825, 1839, and 1849-1851. Each edition is valuable for its preface and additional notes, particularly the last. The Boston printing of 1854 was from the 5th English edition, and included the prefaces of 1819 and 1823. The French edition, *Abrégé de l'histoire d'Angleterre* (Paris, 1827), 10 vols., included an additional preface.

Especially valuable for insight into his historical criticism was John Lingard, *A Vindication of Certain Passages in the Fourth and Fifth Volumes of the History of England*, 2nd ed. (London, 1826). Also used among his minor works were *Remarks on a Charge Delivered to the Clergy of the Diocese of Durham by Shute, Bishop of Durham* (London, 1807); *Collection of Tracts on Several Subjects* (London, 1826), which includes "Documents to Ascertain the Sentiments of British Catholics, in Former Ages, Respecting the Power of the Popes," originally published in 1812; and Thomas Ward, *Errata of the Protestant Bible, to Which are added the Celebrated Preface of the Rev. Dr. Lingard* (New York, 1844). Michael A. Tierney, "Memoir of Rev. Dr. Lingard," the only contemporary biographical sketch of this historian, is included in the sixth edition of the *History of England* (London, 1855), I, pp. 1-42.

Martin Haile and Edwin Bonney, *Life and Letters of John Lingard, 1771-1851* (London, 1911), and Joseph Gillow, ed., *Biographical Dictionary of the English Catholics from the Breach with Rome in 1534 to the Present Time* (London, 1888), 6 vols. include complete lists of Lingard's published works.

Basic also were some two hundred unpublished letters of Dr. Lingard, preserved in the Library of Ushaw College, Durham, and made available to the author by the late Msgr. Philip Hughes. A word of identification of the most consistent of his correspondents may be helpful. John Coulston was Lingard's banker and close friend in Lancaster. The Reverend Robert Gradwell, an author in his own right, was Rector of the English College in Rome, where he served as one of Lingard's "research correspondents"; in 1828 Gradwell was named coadjutor bishop of the London District. An "accomplished antiquary" in scholarship, Francis C. Husenbeth remained a "priest of the old school." Of all of Lingard's correspondents, the most learned and author of several volumes of hagiography was the Reverend John Kirk. The non-Catholic publisher of the various editions of the *History* and an increasingly close friend was Joseph Mawman of London. George Oliver, closely affiliated with the Jesuits, was the well-known historian of Exeter and Devon and frequent contributor to Catholic periodicals. Bishop William Poynter, a moderate opponent of Milner, was the sole member of the hierarchy with whom the vicar of Hornby was on consistently close terms. His main confidant was, however, the canon of Scarborough, John Walker. Significantly, virtually all of Lingard's regular correspondents were English diocesan priests; Charles Butler, the prominent liberal Catholic layman, and Protestants appear but were clearly a minority.

Also valuable for Lingard's historiographical setting were the works and letters of his leading contemporaries, particularly Lord Henry Brougham, Charles Butler, Thomas Carlyle, William Cobbett, Henry Hallam, David Hume, Lord Thomas Macaulay, and Sharon Turner. No less, those of his rather immediate successors provided insights and comparisons: Lord John Dalberg-Acton, Edward A. Freeman, James A. Froude, and John R. Green. Leopold von Ranke's *History of the Latin and Germanic Peoples* (London, 1909), *History of the Popes* (London, 1927), *History of the Reformation in Germany* (New York, 1905), and *History of England Principally in the Seventeenth Century* (New York, 1966) provided the basis of chapter VI.

Finally, the leading contemporary reviews and periodicals furnished much on Lingard's writings as well as their historiographical and social setting. The *Edinburgh Review* was not only the leading Whig organ, but was the particular vehicle of Lord Macaulay, while the Tory view found expression in the *Quarterly Review*. The *Westminster Review* was generally Benthamite in its stance. The *North British Review* and *Blackwood's Edinburgh Magazine* were two lesser rivals, Whig and Tory respectively. The *British Critic* was edited in Lingard's time by an unusually aggressive Anglican, Edward Smedley, whose successor, interestingly, was John Henry Newman. Among the leading periodicals the only Catholic one was the *Dublin Review*, to which Lingard, Wiseman and others regularly contributed.

INDEX